THE ART OF LOVE

KEY TO MEANINGFULL REALATIONSHIPS

Dedication

To my dearest mother, whose love, sacrifices, and unwavering support have shaped my journey. Your strength and wisdom have been my guiding light.

And to my beloved partner, the heart that beats with mine, my source of inspiration and endless encouragement. Your presence makes every challenge worthwhile.

With love and gratitude, this book is for you.

Contents

Introduction: The Purpose of This Book on the Laws of Love

In a world where love often feels elusive and relationships can be fraught with challenges, the quest for understanding love becomes essential. The purpose of this book is to explore the profound nature of love and to illuminate the principles that can transform our relationships into sources of joy, fulfillment, and strength.

At its core, love is not merely an emotion; it is a powerful force that shapes our lives and connects us deeply to one another. Yet, many of us find ourselves navigating love without a clear roadmap. This book aims to provide that guidance, revealing the fundamental laws of love that govern successful relationships.

By understanding what love truly is and how it operates, we can learn to cultivate stronger and happier connections with our partners. We will delve into simple yet transformative practices that can be woven into our daily lives, helping us to nurture our relationships and foster a deeper sense of intimacy and trust.

Through relatable anecdotes, insightful reflections, and practical advice, this book invites you on a journey of discovery. You will learn how to communicate effectively, resolve conflicts with compassion, and create a loving environment that allows both partners to thrive.

Ultimately, the goal is not just to understand love, but to actively learn how to embody it. By embracing these laws and applying them in our relationships, we can build a foundation of love that withstands the test of time, creating bonds that are not only resilient but also immensely rewarding.

Join me as we embark on this exploration of love—its mysteries, its challenges, and its unparalleled joys. Together, we will unlock the secrets to nurturing lasting love, paving the way for a life filled with connection, happiness, and growth.

Motivation Behind Writing This Book

The inspiration to write this book stems from a deeply personal place—my own journey through love. Every experience, every moment of joy and heartache, has shaped my understanding of what love truly means. It is this profound connection to my own story, and the love of my life, that drives me to share these insights with others.

Love is a powerful force that influences our choices, shapes our identities, and enriches our lives. Through my experiences, I have come to realize that love is not just about the grand gestures; it is often found in the small, everyday moments that create lasting memories. These moments—filled with laughter, vulnerability, and growth—have taught me invaluable lessons about trust, communication, and compassion.

As I navigated the complexities of relationships, I encountered challenges that tested my resilience and commitment. Each struggle became a stepping stone, leading me to profound realizations about myself and my partner. I learned that love is a journey,' one that requires continuous effort and

understanding. It is this journey that I wish to share, in hopes that others can find guidance and encouragement along their own paths.

This book is not just a collection of theories or principles; it is a heartfelt exploration of love through my eyes. It reflects my belief that love can be nurtured and strengthened by embracing simplicity and authenticity. By sharing my story, I hope to create a sense of relatability, showing that while each love story is unique, the emotions and challenges we face are universal.

Ultimately, my motivation is to inspire others to recognize the beauty in their own relationships, to cherish the little moments, and to understand that love can be both a refuge and a source of growth. Through this book, I aim to illuminate the path to a deeper, more fulfilling love—one that brings happiness not just to ourselves, but to those we cherish most.

Let us embark on this journey together, discovering the timeless laws of love that can transform our relationships and enrich our lives.

The Transformative Power of Understanding the Laws of Love

Understanding the laws of love is not just an intellectual exercise; it is a transformative journey that can profoundly impact our relationships and, ultimately, our lives. When we grasp these fundamental principles, we unlock the potential to cultivate deeper connections, foster genuine understanding, and create lasting happiness.

At its core, love is a dynamic force that thrives on clarity and intention. By understanding its laws, we gain insights into the nuances of our emotions and the behaviors that shape our relationships. This knowledge empowers us to navigate challenges with grace, communicate more effectively, and build trust. It allows us to see our partners not just as individuals, but as integral parts of a shared journey.

When we apply these laws, we begin to notice remarkable changes. Conflicts that once felt insurmountable can be resolved with empathy and patience. Small misunderstandings can be transformed into opportunities for growth and deeper connection. Love evolves from a mere feeling to a conscious choice—one that we nurture through our actions, words, and intentions.

This transformative power is relatable to anyone who has experienced the ups and downs of relationships. We all know the pain of miscommunication or the heartache of unmet expectations. However, when we understand the underlying principles of love, we can shift our perspectives. We learn that love requires effort and mindfulness, and that every challenge presents an opportunity to strengthen our bond.

Moreover, these laws remind us that love is not just about receiving but also about giving. By embracing the principles of love, we cultivate an environment where both partners feel valued and heard. This mutual respect and understanding lay the foundation for a resilient relationship, capable of weathering any storm.

Ultimately, the laws of love serve as a guide, illuminating the path toward a fulfilling and joyful partnership. They remind us that love is not a destination, but a continuous journey of growth and discovery. As we embrace these principles, we create space for authentic connection, joy, and lasting happiness in our relationships.

Join me in exploring the transformative power of understanding the laws of love. Together, we can unlock the secrets to nurturing our relationships and building a life filled with connection, warmth, and profound love.

Embracing the Journey of Love: A Reflection on Connection

This book explores the profound laws that govern love relationships, illuminating the path to deeper connections and enduring bonds. Each chapter serves as a guide to nurture and strengthen the vital elements of a successful partnership. From the foundations of communication and respect to the transformative power of forgiveness and growth, this work invites readers to embark on a journey toward love's truest expression.

As you delve into these pages, take a moment to reflect on your own relationships. Are there areas where you can deepen your understanding or enhance your connection? This book encourages you to explore your feelings, challenge assumptions, and embrace the beauty of vulnerability.

With relatable insights and practical wisdom, each chapter invites you to consider how these laws can reshape your love life. Whether you're in a long-term partnership or seeking to enrich your understanding of love, this journey is for you. Let the transformative power of these laws guide you toward a more fulfilling and authentic connection. Together, let's uncover the beauty of love, one law at a time.

Embrace the adventure of love—your heart will thank you.

1. The Symphony of Communication
- "In every word, a bridge; in every silence, a pause."

Communication serves as the golden thread that binds hearts together. It is more than just exchanging words; it's the art of sharing thoughts, emotions, and vulnerabilities. In a world where silence can often speak louder than words, the true essence of communication in love lies in its ability to foster connection and understanding. Imagine two lovers standing on opposite shores of a vast ocean. Without the bridge of communication, they are isolated, their thoughts and feelings lost in the waves. Yet, when they share their hopes, fears, dreams, and disappointments, they create a path that draws them closer, transcending distance and time. This connection not only nurtures the bond between them but also paves the way for trust and intimacy. Effective communication in love means listening as much as speaking. It's about creating a safe space where both partners feel valued and heard. When we truly listen, we validate each other's experiences and emotions, allowing love to flourish in the fertile ground of mutual respect. However, communication in love is not always easy. Misunderstandings can arise, and emotions can run high. Yet, it is during these challenging moments that love's true strength is tested. Embracing vulnerability and approaching conflicts with compassion transforms challenges into opportunities for growth, deepening the relationship. As we embark on this exploration of the laws of love, let us recognize that communication is not merely a skill but a lifelong journey. It requires patience, practice, and a commitment to understanding one another. Together, let's uncover the beautiful nuances of love's language and discover how mastering this art can lead to deeper connections, enriched experiences, and a love that stands the test of time.

A Love Rekindled: The Story of Aarav and Meera

In the bustling heart of Delhi, where the cacophony of life intertwines with the whispers of romance, Aarav and Meera found each other amidst the chaos. Their love story began in a quaint café in Connaught Place, where the aroma of freshly brewed coffee mingled with the sound of laughter. They were young, carefree, and enchanted by the possibility of a future together.

As they strolled hand-in-hand through the vibrant streets, every shared glance and gentle touch felt electric. Their evenings were filled with deep conversations under starlight skies, dreams painted in vivid colors, and plans for adventures yet to come. In those early days, love was a beautiful symphony, each note resonating with passion and joy.

However, as time passed and life became busier, the melody began to falter. Aarav's job demanded long hours, and Meera found herself engrossed in her studies. They drifted into a routine, their conversations reduced to mundane exchanges about the day. The spark that once ignited their hearts now flickered uncertainly.

The turning point came one chilly evening when they sat on a bench at India Gate, wrapped in silence. Meera could feel the distance between them, a chasm widening with every unspoken word. "Aarav, do you feel it too?" she finally asked, her voice barely above a whisper.

Aarav sighed, his heart heavy with unexpressed feelings. "I do, Meera. It feels like we're living parallel lives. I miss us."

In that moment of vulnerability, they realized that the root of their struggles was a lack of communication. They had both been holding back, afraid to share their fears and frustrations. The love that had once flowed freely now felt stifled, trapped beneath layers of unexpressed emotions.

Determined to bridge the gap, they made a pact to communicate openly. They decided to set aside time each week, free from distractions, to talk about their feelings, dreams, and worries. It wasn't always easy; some conversations were uncomfortable, filled with tears and moments of doubt. Yet, each exchange became a stepping stone toward healing.

As they began to open up, Meera shared her anxiety about her upcoming exams, while Aarav expressed the pressures he felt at work. They discovered that by voicing their fears, they could support each other, creating a safe space where both felt valued and understood.

Their relationship transformed before their eyes. The laughter returned, accompanied by deeper discussions that reignited their emotional connection. They found joy in the simple act of being vulnerable with one another, their bond growing stronger with each conversation. Weekend picnics turned into heart-to-heart talks under the shade of trees, and late-night drives became opportunities for sharing dreams.

One evening, as they sat on their favorite bench, now adorned with the memories of their journey, Aarav took Meera's hand. "I never realized how important communication was until we faced the silence," he said, looking into her eyes. "It's like we've rediscovered each other."

Meera smiled, her heart swelling with love. "We've learned that love isn't just about the good times. It's about being there for each other, even in the tough moments."

Their story, once tinged with uncertainty, blossomed into a beautiful narrative of growth and resilience. The streets of Delhi, once mere backdrops to their love, now pulsed with the rhythm of their renewed connection. They learned that communication is not just a skill but the very foundation of love—a bridge that brings two hearts closer, no matter the distance.

As seasons changed, so did Aarav and Meera. Their relationship became a testament to the power of open dialogue, reminding them that true love thrives in honesty and vulnerability. Together, they crafted a love story that was not just beautiful but deeply relatable—a reminder that communication can transform love, making it richer and more profound.

The Heart of Connection: How Communication Fosters Understanding in Love

In the intricate dance of love, communication acts as the guiding rhythm, ensuring that both partners move in harmony. Aarav and Meera's journey illustrates a fundamental truth: clear and open communication fosters connection while preventing misunderstandings.

Building Bridges, Not Walls

When Aarav and Meera first fell in love, their communication was effortless—a natural flow of thoughts and emotions. As they grew busier, however, silence crept in, creating distance between them. This illustrates a crucial point: when we stop communicating, we unintentionally build walls that isolate us.

By openly expressing their feelings and concerns, Aarav and Meera learned to dismantle these walls, allowing for a deeper connection to flourish.

The Power of Vulnerability

Effective communication requires vulnerability. When Meera voiced her anxieties about her exams and Aarav shared his work pressures, they each took a risk, exposing their fears. This act of vulnerability is vital in relationships; it invites understanding and empathy. Instead of feeling alone in their struggles, they found solace in each other, reinforcing their bond. Vulnerability transforms potential conflicts into opportunities for growth and intimacy.

Clarifying Intentions and Emotions

Misunderstandings often arise from assumptions. Aarav and Meera initially assumed they understood each other's feelings, leading to frustration and disconnection. Through their dedicated time for conversation, they clarified their intentions and emotions, transforming ambiguity into clarity. This practice not only prevented misunderstandings but also fostered a culture of honesty in their relationship.

Active Listening: The Key to Connection

A critical component of effective communication is active listening. Aarav and Meera discovered that listening goes beyond hearing words; it involves truly understanding the feelings behind them. When they practiced active listening, they validated each other's experiences, which deepened their emotional connection. This mutual understanding became the foundation for their love, creating a safe space where both felt valued and accepted.

Transforming Conflict into Collaboration

Every relationship faces challenges, but how we communicate during these times can make all the difference. Aarav and Meera's commitment to open dialogue transformed potential conflicts into collaborative problem-solving. Rather than allowing disagreements to drive them apart, they embraced these moments as opportunities to strengthen their bond. Their willingness to communicate openly turned conflicts into a joint effort to understand and support one another.

The Ripple Effect of Connection

The positive effects of effective communication extend beyond the couple. As Aarav and Meera grew closer through their discussions, their friends and family also noticed a change. Their renewed connection radiated warmth and positivity, creating a ripple effect that enriched their relationships with others. When communication flourishes in a romantic relationship, it often inspires those around to communicate more openly as well.

The Lifeblood of Love

In Aarav and Meera's story, we see how communication is not just a tool but the very lifeblood of love. It fosters connection, prevents misunderstandings, and transforms challenges into growth opportunities. As we navigate our own relationships, let us remember that open dialogue and active listening are essential in cultivating deep, meaningful connections. By embracing the power of communication, we can create a love that not only withstands the test of time but thrives in its warmth.

Research has consistently shown that communication plays a crucial role in relationship

satisfaction. Here are some key statistics and findings related to this topic:

1. **Positive Communication and Satisfaction** : According to a study published in the Journal of Marriage and Family, couples who engage in positive communication—such as expressing appreciation, affection, and respect—report higher levels of relationship satisfaction.

2. **Conflict Resolution** : Research from the American Psychological Association indicates that couples who utilize constructive communication strategies during conflicts are more likely to experience relationship satisfaction compared to those who engage in negative communication patterns (e.g., criticism, defensiveness).

3. **Listening Skills** : A study published in the Journal of Social and Personal Relationships found that active listening significantly correlates with relationship satisfaction. Couples who practiced active listening reported feeling more understood and connected.

4. **Emotional Intimacy** : Research in the Journal of Family Psychology highlights that open communication about emotions leads to greater emotional intimacy, which in turn is linked to overall relationship satisfaction.

5. **Communication Frequency** : According to a study published in Personal Relationships, couples who communicate frequently about their daily lives and feelings report higher relationship satisfaction. This frequency helps maintain emotional closeness.

6. **Avoiding Withdrawal** : A study from the International Journal of Psychology found that couples who avoid withdrawing from conversations during conflicts tend to have

more satisfying relationships. Withdrawal often leads to unresolved issues and feelings of disconnect.

7. **Predictive Power** : Research from the Gottman Institute suggests that communication patterns can predict relationship longevity. Couples who engage in negative communication styles (e.g., stonewalling, contempt) are more likely to face relationship dissatisfaction over time.

8. **Gender Differences** : A study published in Gender Roles found that men and women may have different communication styles, which can affect relationship satisfaction. Understanding and adapting to these differences can lead to improved satisfaction for both partners.

9. **Impact of Technology** : Research shows that while technology can facilitate communication, it can also create misunderstandings if misused. A study in the Journal of Communication indicates that excessive reliance on text-based communication can lead to reduced relationship satisfaction due to lack of non-verbal cues.

Conclusion: The Power of Communication in Love

As we close this chapter on the essential role of communication in love, let's take a moment to reflect on the journey we've embarked upon together. Communication is not merely the exchange of words; it is the heartbeat of a thriving relationship, the bridge that connects two souls navigating the complexities of life together.

In the world of love, where emotions ebb and flow like the tides, effective communication serves as our anchor. It empowers us to express our deepest feelings, to share our dreams, and to address our fears. Through the stories of Aarav and Meera, we've seen how open dialogue can turn misunderstandings into moments of connection, transforming challenges into opportunities for growth.

But the beauty of communication lies not just in the spoken word; it resides in the silent understanding, the gentle nod, and the shared laughter. It invites us to be vulnerable, to listen deeply, and to cherish the moments that bind us. Remember, every conversation is a chance to deepen your connection, to build trust, and to nurture the love you share.

As you move forward, carry these insights into your own relationships. Embrace the practice of open dialogue, cultivate the art of active listening, and cherish the moments of vulnerability. The journey of love is a continuous exploration, and each conversation is a stepping stone toward a richer, more fulfilling partnership.

So, let your heart be open and your words be kind. As you turn the page to the next chapter, know that the power of communication is in your hands—ready to enhance your love story in ways you never imagined. Here's to a future filled with understanding, connection, and the beautiful language of love. Let's continue this journey together!

2. The Art of Conflict Resolution

- "In every conflict, an opportunity for deeper understanding."

Conflict is an inevitable part of any relationship, including love relationships. Disagreements and differences are natural, given that two people come from distinct backgrounds, have unique personalities, and hold diverse perspectives. The key to maintaining a healthy and enduring relationship lies in how couples handle conflicts. Instead of allowing disagreements to escalate into destructive arguments, couples who understand and employ healthy conflict resolution strategies can strengthen their bond, deepen their understanding of each other, and enhance their connection.

In this chapter, we'll explore healthy strategies for conflict resolution that can help couples navigate disagreements constructively. We'll introduce several techniques—such as time-outs, scheduling discussions, and active listening—that encourage respect, understanding, and growth during times of tension.

Conflict Resolution – A Love Rekindled

Aishwarya and Ravi had been in a relationship for nearly four years. Their love story was one of serendipity — two souls who met by chance at a mutual friend's wedding in the picturesque city of Mysore, their hometown. Aishwarya, with her sparkling eyes and deep sense of empathy, immediately captured Ravi's heart. Ravi, on the other hand, was a reserved and thoughtful young man, whose warmth emerged through his gentle actions. Together, they had built a life that seemed perfect in the eyes of everyone around them.

But as with all relationships, love alone was not enough to shield them from the inevitable conflicts that arose. What started as small disagreements soon spiraled into more frequent and intense arguments. Aishwarya, who was emotionally expressive, often felt misunderstood. Ravi, though deeply loving, was not as open about his feelings, and his silence in the face of conflict created a distance that neither of them had anticipated. The gap between them began to widen, and both were left wondering if they could ever bridge it.

The Breaking Point

It all came to a head one rainy evening, the kind of evening that Mysore is known for — calm, serene, with the smell of wet earth hanging in the air. They were at their favorite café in the city center, an old and cozy place where they had shared many memories. But tonight, the air between them was heavy. Aishwarya had recently received a promotion at work, and Ravi, who had always been supportive of her ambitions, had grown distant. The reason was simple, yet unspoken — he was struggling with his own sense of stagnation at work, and instead of confiding in Aishwarya, he allowed jealousy to fester.

Ravi, why are you so quiet? You haven't said a word since we got here," Aishwarya finally broke the silence, frustration creeping into her voice.

Ravi, staring down at his coffee cup, didn't look up. "I'm fine, Aishwarya. Why do you always have to make a big deal out of everything?"

Aishwarya's heart sank. The words felt like a slap, but she knew Ravi well enough to understand that this was more than just an offhand remark. He was hurt. And she was hurt too, but the difference was she wore her feelings on her sleeve, while he bottled them up.

"Why can't you just talk to me? Tell me what's bothering you instead of shutting me out!" Her voice shook with emotion.

Ravi's face tightened, and for a moment, they both sat in silence, the weight of unsaid words heavy between them. The café seemed to grow quieter as their argument escalated. Aishwarya's chest tightened, and she could feel the familiar sting of tears threatening to spill over. But she refused to let them fall. Not here, not now.

"I can't keep doing this, Ravi," she whispered, her voice barely audible over the sound of the rain tapping against the windows. "I can't keep fighting like this and not even know why. I love you, but I can't keep trying to fix everything on my own."

Ravi's eyes, which had been avoiding hers for the longest time, finally met hers. The pain in his gaze was undeniable. "I don't know what to do, Aishwarya. I don't know how to deal with what I'm feeling. And I hate that I'm making you feel like this."

Aishwarya took a deep breath. This wasn't just about the fight anymore; it was about the gap they had let form between them. And at that moment, Aishwarya knew that if they didn't address it now, their love might slowly slip away.

A Turning Point

They didn't speak for the rest of the evening. But the silence was different — it wasn't the uncomfortable silence of unresolved tension. It was the silence that came after understanding, after realizing that something had to change.

That night, Aishwarya stayed up long after Ravi had gone to bed. She thought about all the times they had argued — how their voices had grown louder, their words sharper, until the very thing they had once cherished began to feel fragile. She remembered the early days of their relationship, when they had spoken for hours about everything and nothing, their hearts open and vulnerable.

She knew something had to change, but it couldn't be just her doing all the changing. Ravi had to be part of this too.

The Resolution

The next day, Aishwarya approached Ravi in the calm of the morning, before the weight of the day could steal their time together. She had thought long and hard about this moment, and she knew this had to be the start of something different.

"Ravi, I know we've been struggling lately, but I don't want us to keep drifting apart," she began gently. "I've been thinking... we need to learn how to talk to each other in a way that helps, not hurts. And I'm willing to try if you are."

Ravi looked at her, his face softened with a mixture of regret and love. "I'm sorry, Aishwarya. I didn't mean to pull away from you. I guess... I guess I didn't know how to handle my own feelings. I was afraid that you would think less of me if I told you how I was feeling."

Aishwarya smiled, a little tear escaping her eye. "I don't want you to be afraid to tell me anything. We're partners, Ravi. We're supposed to help each other through everything — even the difficult parts."

They both agreed on one thing: they needed a new approach to conflict resolution — one that didn't involve raising voices, holding grudges, or giving each other the cold shoulder.

Healthy Conflict Resolution Techniques

Time-Outs: They decided to introduce the concept of time-outs into their relationship. The next time they felt the argument escalating, they would pause, step back, and take a break to collect their thoughts. This gave them both the space to cool down and avoid saying things they didn't mean in the heat of the moment.

Scheduled Discussions: Rather than letting frustrations build up until they exploded, they agreed to schedule regular times to check in with each other. Every weekend, they would sit down with a cup of coffee and talk about how they were feeling, what had been bothering them, and what they could do to make each other's lives better. No phones, no distractions — just undivided attention.

Active Listening: Ravi learned how to listen actively to Aishwarya, and Aishwarya, in turn, became more patient with Ravi's silent moments. They practiced reflecting back what they heard, not as an interrogation, but as a way to ensure they truly understood each other's perspectives.

Empathy and Forgiveness: They learned to approach each other's emotions with empathy, rather than defensiveness. If one of them felt hurt, the other would listen without judgment. And when mistakes were made, they embraced the power of forgiveness — acknowledging the pain, accepting responsibility, and moving forward together.

A New Beginning

Months passed, and with each passing day, Aishwarya and Ravi grew closer. Their conflicts, though still present, became opportunities for growth. They no longer saw disagreements as threats, but as challenges to overcome together. They realized that the strength of their love was not measured by the absence of conflict, but by their ability to resolve it with respect, understanding, and a shared commitment to each other.

One quiet evening, as they walked hand-in-hand along the Brindavan Gardens, the setting sun casting a golden glow on the water, Aishwarya looked up at Ravi and smiled.

"We've come a long way, haven't we?" she said.

Ravi squeezed her hand gently, his heart full. "Yes, we have. And I'll keep doing the work, Aishwarya. For us."

Aishwarya smiled back, knowing that no matter the challenges life might bring, they had learned the most important lesson: **love isn't just about the good times, but about how you resolve the bad ones together.**

And that, they both knew, was what truly mattered.

The Importance of Respectful Disagreements in Love Relationships

Disagreements in relationships are inevitable. No matter how compatible two people are, there will always be moments when they don't see eye to eye. However, the way these disagreements are handled can either make or break a relationship. Respectful disagreements are a critical aspect of conflict resolution, particularly in romantic relationships. They allow partners to express their differing views without damaging the relationship or causing emotional harm. The key lies in approaching conflicts in a way that prioritizes understanding, empathy, and mutual respect.

Respectful disagreements are not about avoiding conflict altogether; instead, they focus on handling disagreements constructively. This approach fosters personal growth, emotional intimacy, and stronger bonds between partners. When handled well, disagreements can even strengthen the relationship, making both individuals more understanding of each other's needs and perspectives.

Why Respectful Disagreements Matter

Preserves Emotional Safety

When conflicts are approached with respect, both partners feel safe expressing their feelings, fears, and frustrations. This emotional safety allows both individuals to be vulnerable, which deepens intimacy and strengthens trust. If disagreements escalate into personal attacks or hurtful language, it can cause lasting emotional wounds that take time to heal, or worse, create resentment that slowly erodes the foundation of the relationship.

Promotes Constructive Resolution

Respectful disagreements focus on resolving the issue at hand rather than on "winning" the argument. When both partners maintain respect for each other, they can focus on the solution instead of getting stuck in blame or defensiveness.

This leads to more effective problem-solving and better outcomes in the long run.

Encourages Growth and Understanding

Every disagreement is an opportunity to learn something new about your partner. Respectful disagreements help foster a deeper understanding of each other's values, perspectives, and needs. By approaching a conflict with an open mind and a willingness to listen, both partners can grow individually and as a couple.

Strengthens the Relationship

Healthy conflict resolution strengthens relationships, as it allows both partners to feel heard and understood. Over time, this creates a sense of partnership where both individuals are invested in not just "getting their way," but in nurturing the relationship and finding solutions that work for both people.

Embracing the Art of Conflict Resolution

Conflict is an inherent part of any relationship, but it doesn't have to be a source of division or pain. In fact, when approached with intention, empathy, and respect, conflict can become a powerful opportunity for growth, deeper connection, and mutual understanding. The key lies not in avoiding disagreements, but in how we navigate them.

In this chapter, we've explored the tools and techniques that can help transform conflict from a destructive force into a constructive one. We've learned that de-escalation starts with self-awareness, and that listening—truly listening—is the cornerstone of any meaningful conversation. By speaking from a place of respect, owning our emotions, and focusing on the issue rather than the person, we create an environment where both partners feel heard, valued, and understood.

The ability to resolve conflict healthily requires practice, patience, and a commitment to the relationship. It means learning to pause when emotions run high, using soothing language to calm the situation, and actively choosing to respond, not react. It's about recognizing that disagreement doesn't equate to disconnection, but rather an invitation to come closer—to refine, clarify, and strengthen the bond you share.

By embracing these conflict resolution strategies, you are not just learning to "solve problems"—you are learning to create a space where both partners can thrive. In every conflict lies the potential for deeper intimacy, clearer communication, and a more resilient partnership. Each disagreement becomes a moment to reaffirm your commitment to each other, to show that love isn't about perfection, but about patience, respect, and the willingness to grow together.

As you move forward, remember that conflicts, when handled with care, can become the threads that weave a stronger, more resilient relationship. They teach us about ourselves, our partners, and the delicate art of love itself. With these tools in hand, you have everything you need to turn conflict into opportunity—an opportunity to nurture a relationship grounded in understanding, trust, and mutual respect.

3. The Pillar of Respect

- "Respect: the foundation where love finds its strength."

Respect is the heartbeat of any loving relationship. It goes beyond mere tolerance; it's about recognizing and valuing your partner's individuality, thoughts, and emotions. In essence, respect means treating your partner as an equal, honoring their feelings, and acknowledging their worth. This mutual appreciation lays the groundwork for a thriving connection.

In daily interactions, respect manifests in countless ways. It's in the way you listen—truly listen—when your partner speaks, making them feel heard and understood. It's about valuing their opinions, even when they differ from your own, and engaging in constructive discussions rather than dismissive arguments. Small gestures, like asking about their day or remembering their preferences, show that you care and are invested in their happiness.

Respect also involves honoring boundaries—recognizing when your partner needs space or time for themselves. It's about supporting their dreams and aspirations, encouraging them to pursue their passions without judgment or doubt. In moments of conflict, it means addressing issues with kindness, avoiding hurtful words, and seeking to understand rather than to win.

Ultimately, respect creates a nurturing environment where both partners can flourish. As we delve into this chapter, we'll explore practical ways to cultivate respect in your relationship, reinforcing its vital role in building a love that is not only deep but also resilient. Through respect, we transform love from a fleeting feeling into a lasting bond, empowering both partners to grow together.

The Journey of Aisha and Raj: Learning the Power of Respect

In the vibrant city of Mumbai, Aisha and Raj embarked on their journey as a newly married couple, filled with dreams and love. The bustling streets and endless energy of the city mirrored their excitement, but as the days turned into weeks, they soon encountered the reality of their new life together.

At first, everything seemed perfect. Aisha loved Raj's ambition, while he admired her creativity and warmth. However, as they settled into daily routines, the honeymoon phase began to fade. Small disagreements about household chores and finances spiraled into bigger conflicts. Aisha often felt that Raj dismissed her opinions, particularly about how to manage their budget, while Raj struggled to understand Aisha's need for more quality time, believing her creative pursuits took precedence over their relationship.

One evening, after a particularly heated argument, Aisha sat alone on their balcony, watching the city lights flicker against the night sky. She felt a deep sense of frustration and sadness. It wasn't just the disagreement that bothered her; it was the feeling that Raj didn't respect her perspective. In his mind, he was trying to be practical, but in the process, he overlooked her feelings.

That night, Raj found Aisha in tears. Seeing her vulnerability, something shifted within him. He realized that their love, which had once been so joyful, was now clouded by misunderstandings. They sat down together, and for the first time, they truly listened to each other. Aisha shared her dreams and how much she valued being heard, while Raj expressed his own fears of financial instability.

In that moment, they began to understand the heart of their struggles: a lack of respect for one another's thoughts and feelings. They made a pact to prioritize respect in their relationship, committing to listen actively and validate each other's emotions, even in moments of disagreement.

Over the following weeks, Aisha and Raj transformed their interactions. Raj learned to pause and consider Aisha's perspective before responding, while Aisha worked on expressing her feelings without fear of judgment. They started to hold regular 'check-in' conversations, where they could openly discuss their feelings and any issues that arose, ensuring they both felt valued.

One sunny Saturday afternoon, while cooking together, Aisha turned to Raj and said, "I love how we can talk about anything now. It feels like we're really a team." Raj smiled, his heart swelling with pride. He had started to appreciate Aisha's creative ideas, often incorporating them into their plans. Their once-distant conversations were now filled with laughter, respect, and understanding.

As they navigated their daily lives, from bustling market trips to cozy evenings at home, the bond they forged through mutual respect deepened. They celebrated each other's successes, supported one another during challenges, and found joy in the little things—a shared coffee on the balcony or a spontaneous outing to explore the city.

In recognizing the importance of respect, Aisha and Raj not only salvaged their relationship but also transformed it into something beautiful and resilient. They learned that love isn't just about grand gestures; it's about the everyday choices to honor each other as equals.

Their story is a testament to the transformative power of respect in love. Aisha and Raj discovered that by nurturing a culture of respect, they could weather any storm together, ultimately creating a partnership rooted in trust, admiration, and lasting joy. As they walked hand in hand through the bustling streets of Mumbai, they understood that respect wasn't just a rule; it was the very foundation of their love story.

"The Art of Respect: Building a Lasting Love Through Kindness and Connection"

Respect is an essential ingredient in nurturing a loving relationship, and it can be expressed through various means. Verbal affirmations play a significant role; regularly expressing gratitude by thanking your partner for their efforts—whether big or small—can make a world of difference. Phrases like "I appreciate you" or "I understand how you feel" validate your partner's emotions, showing you value their perspective. Encouraging words, such as "You've got this!" or "I believe in you!" can empower your partner and reinforce their self-worth. Alongside verbal communication, using kind words like genuine compliments about their strengths, talents, or appearance creates an atmosphere of warmth and intimacy. Simple statements like "You look amazing today!" or engaging with thoughtful responses during conversations—such as "What do you think about that?"—invites your partner to share their views and feel heard.

Nonverbal cues are equally important in demonstrating respect. Maintaining eye contact during conversations conveys interest and sincerity, showing that you're fully present and invested. Open body language, like facing your partner, uncrossing your arms, and leaning in slightly, communicates receptiveness and approachability. Gentle touches, such as a light hand on their arm, holding hands, or a warm hug, can express respect and affection without the need for words, reinforcing your emotional connection.

To integrate these practices into your daily life, cultivate mindfulness by being aware of your tone and body language in every interaction, approaching discussions with kindness and openness. After disagreements, take time to reflect on how you can improve respect in future conversations, demonstrating a commitment to growth. Establishing rituals, such as sharing a gratitude list or a moment of connection each day or week, can further strengthen respect as a foundation in your relationship. By weaving these practices into your everyday interactions, you not only show respect but also cultivate a deeper, more loving bond with your partner, transforming love into a powerful, lasting connection.

Verbal Affirmations

Express Gratitude: Regularly thank your partner for their efforts, whether big or small. A simple "I appreciate you" can make a world of difference.

Acknowledge Feelings: Use phrases like, "I understand how you feel" or "That makes sense" to validate their emotions, showing you value their perspective.

Encouragement: Offer words of support, such as "You've got this!" or "I believe in you!" to empower your partner and reinforce their self-worth.

Compliments: Compliment your partner's strengths, talents, or appearance genuinely. A heartfelt "You look amazing today!" goes a long way.

Active Listening: Show your engagement by responding thoughtfully during conversations. Phrases like "What do you think about that?" invite your partner to share their views.

Affectionate Language: Use terms of endearment that resonate with both of you, creating an atmosphere of warmth and intimacy.

Nonverbal Cues

Eye Contact: Maintain eye contact during conversations to convey interest and sincerity. It shows you're fully present and invested in what they're saying.

Open Body Language: Face your partner, uncross your arms, and lean in slightly. This posture communicates that you are receptive and approachable.

Touch: A gentle touch on the arm, holding hands, or a warm hug can express respect and affection without words, reinforcing your emotional connection.

Tips for Everyday Practice

Mindfulness: Be aware of your tone and body language in every interaction. Approach discussions with kindness and openness.

Reflect: After disagreements, take time to reflect on how you can improve respect in future conversations. This shows a commitment to growth.

Create Rituals: Establish daily or weekly rituals, like sharing a gratitude list or a moment of connection, to strengthen respect as a foundation in your relationship.

By integrating these practices into your daily life, you not only show respect but also cultivate a deeper, more loving bond with your partner. Remember, respect is not just a feeling; it's an action that transforms love into a powerful, lasting connection.

The Beauty of Boundaries in Love

In any loving relationship, setting and honoring personal boundaries is essential for fostering mutual respect and emotional well-being. Boundaries help define where one person ends and another begins, creating a safe space for both partners to thrive. Here's how to effectively discuss and honor these boundaries, handle disrespect, and engage in calm discussions about feelings.

Discussing and Honoring Personal Boundaries

Open communication is the cornerstone of boundary setting. Begin by sharing your needs and feelings with your partner in a non-confrontational way. Use "I" statements, such as "I feel overwhelmed when my privacy is not respected" rather than placing blame. This approach fosters understanding rather than defensiveness. Encourage your partner to express their own boundaries too, creating a space for open dialogue. Once boundaries are established, honor them consistently. Show commitment by respecting your partner's limits, whether it's about personal space, emotional needs, or time alone. This mutual respect strengthens the bond and builds trust, allowing both partners to feel safe and valued.

Handling Disrespect

Despite the best intentions, misunderstandings can arise, leading to moments of disrespect. When this happens, it's important to address the issue calmly and directly. Approach your partner when emotions are stable, and express how their actions made you feel. Use language that focuses on the behavior, not the person. For example, say, "I felt hurt when my request was ignored," instead of "You never listen." This way, you open the door for dialogue rather than defensiveness. Remember, it's essential to listen to your partner's perspective too, as this fosters understanding and helps you both learn from the experience.

Having Calm Discussions About Feelings

Creating an environment conducive to open discussions about feelings is vital. Choose a comfortable, private space where both partners feel safe to express themselves. Start the conversation with a positive tone, perhaps by expressing gratitude for your partner or acknowledging the good in your relationship. When discussing feelings, use "I" statements to articulate your emotions clearly. For instance, "I feel anxious when plans change last minute" communicates your feelings without sounding accusatory. Invite your partner to share their feelings in return, and practice active listening—give them your full attention, maintain eye contact, and validate their emotions, even if you don't agree. This respectful exchange not only resolves issues but also deepens intimacy and connection.

By embracing the practice of setting boundaries, handling disrespect thoughtfully, and engaging in calm discussions about feelings, you create a nurturing and supportive environment. This framework not only helps you navigate challenges but also strengthens your relationship, allowing love to flourish in a space where both partners feel respected and valued. In the journey of love, boundaries are not walls; they are bridges that connect two hearts, fostering deeper understanding and lasting joy.

Embracing Respect in Love

As we conclude this chapter on respect in love, it becomes clear that respect is not merely a guideline; it is the essence of a thriving relationship. When we choose to honor each other's feelings, boundaries, and individuality, we create a nurturing environment where love can flourish. Respect lays the foundation for trust, intimacy, and genuine connection, transforming our relationships into vibrant partnerships filled with joy and understanding.

Imagine embarking on a journey where each day is an opportunity to deepen your bond, to truly see and appreciate one another. By integrating respect into your daily interactions, you open the door to a richer, more fulfilling love story—one where both partners feel valued and empowered.

So, as you take your next steps, remember that this journey is not just about the destination; it's about the moments you share and the respect you cultivate along the way. Embrace the challenges and triumphs, and let respect be your guiding star.

We encourage you to continue exploring the laws of love, armed with the knowledge that respect is the heartbeat of your connection. May your relationship be filled with kindness, understandin mutual appreciation. Here's to the exciting adventure ahead—happy reading and even happier loving!

37

4. The Essence of Trust

- "Trust is the quiet certainty that love can flourish."

In the intricate dance of love, trust serves as the steadfast rhythm that keeps partners in harmony. Like the foundation of a grand building, trust is essential; without it, everything above risks collapsing. Trust isn't merely an absence of doubt; it's a vibrant, living force that nurtures connection, fosters intimacy, and creates a safe space for vulnerability.

Consider trust as the glue that binds hearts together. It allows us to share our innermost thoughts and feelings without fear of judgment or betrayal. When we trust, we can be our authentic selves, revealing both our strengths and our insecurities. This openness enriches the relationship, transforming it into a sanctuary where love can flourish.

However, trust is not a static entity; it requires nurturing, patience, and, at times, repair. Just as a garden needs water and sunlight, trust thrives on communication, honesty, and shared experiences. It grows stronger through acts of kindness and deepens through understanding. When challenges arise, it's the commitment to rebuild and reconnect that fortifies the bond, reminding us that love is not just about perfection but also about perseverance.

In the following pages, we will explore how to cultivate trust in our relationships, the role of vulnerability, and how to navigate the inevitable storms that test our bonds. Together, we'll uncover the transformative power of trust, revealing how it can elevate love from mere affection to an unshakeable partnership. Let us embark on this journey, where trust becomes the bedrock upon which lasting love is built.

Trust in Love: A Bangalore Tale

In the bustling heart of Bangalore, where the aroma of fresh coffee mingles with the sound of honking rickshaws, lived Aditi and Rohan, a couple whose love story seemed to mirror the vibrant city around them. They had met during a poetry reading at a quaint café in Indiranagar, where words flowed like the gentle breeze. Their connection was instant, built on shared dreams and laughter.

As their relationship blossomed, so did their shared adventures—weekend getaways to Nandi Hills, late-night drives through the illuminated streets, and countless hours spent lost in conversation. However, beneath this picturesque exterior, trust issues began to cast shadows on their love. Rohan, with his charismatic charm, had a circle of friends that often included old flames. Aditi found herself grappling with insecurities, feeling like she was competing with memories that refused to fade.

One rainy evening, after a particularly heated argument about Rohan's late-night outings, Aditi sat alone on their balcony, the rain mirroring her turmoil. She felt a mix of frustration and heartbreak, wondering if their love was strong enough to weather these storms. Rohan joined her, sensing the tension in the air. As they sipped their steaming cups of chai, he reached for her hand, a silent plea for understanding.

"Aditi," he began, his voice steady yet vulnerable. "I can see the doubts in your eyes. I never want to be the cause of your pain. Can we talk about this?"

With tears welling up, Aditi opened up about her fears and insecurities. She spoke of the sleepless nights and the gnawing thoughts that haunted her, even when they were together. Rohan listened intently, his heart aching for the woman he loved. He realized that while he valued his friendships, he had inadvertently created a distance between them by not being transparent about his interactions.

"I never meant to hurt you," he admitted, his sincerity cutting through the tension. "Let's build a new foundation—one built on trust. I want you to feel secure with me."

That night marked a turning point. They began to establish an unspoken rule: honesty above all. Rohan agreed to share more about his life outside their relationship, while Aditi committed to voicing her feelings rather than bottling them up. They created a safe space, free of judgment, where vulnerability became their strongest asset.

As weeks turned into months, their bond deepened. They would often sit on their balcony, sharing their daily triumphs and struggles. Aditi learned to appreciate Rohan's friendships as part of his journey, while he became her anchor, reassuring her that his heart was firmly anchored in their love. They celebrated each other's successes, big and small, and faced challenges hand in hand.

One evening, as they strolled through Cubbon Park, Aditi took Rohan's hand and whispered, "Thank you for choosing to trust me and for letting me trust you." Rohan smiled, knowing that they had not only weathered the storm but emerged stronger together. Trust had transformed their relationship from one marred by insecurity to a love grounded in mutual respect and understanding.

Their story, like Bangalore itself, was a blend of chaos and beauty. Through the lens of trust, they learned that love is not just about perfection; it's about navigating imperfections together. And in that journey, they discovered that their relationship was a masterpiece, painted with colors of honesty, vulnerability, and unwavering trust.

As Aditi and Rohan continued to write their love story, they realized that trust wasn't merely a rule but a guiding principle that would lead them through life's many adventures. Together, they forged a love that was not just beautiful, but beautifully resilient.

The Role of Consistency and Reliability in Fostering Trust

In any relationship, trust serves as the cornerstone, built gradually through consistent actions and reliable behaviors. Just as a bank account thrives on careful deposits, so too does trust flourish when partners consistently invest in one another. This concept can be vividly illustrated through the "trust bank" metaphor—a powerful framework for understanding how our actions impact the trust we build with our loved ones.

The Trust Bank

Imagine your relationship as a trust bank, where every positive interaction is a deposit, and every breach of trust or inconsistency is a withdrawal. Each time you show up for your partner, offer a listening ear, or keep a promise, you are making a deposit. These small yet meaningful acts accumulate over time, creating a strong foundation of trust. Just as a bank account grows with each deposit, so too does trust flourish with every demonstration of reliability.

Conversely, when trust is compromised—be it through broken promises, lack of communication, or inconsistent behavior—it results in a withdrawl. Each time trust is undermined, it diminishes the balance of your trust bank, leaving your relationship vulnerable. If these withdrawals exceed your deposits, the relationship can become precarious, creating an atmosphere of doubt and insecurity.

Building a Healthy Trust Bank

To foster trust, consistency and reliability must become cornerstones of your relationship. Here are some practical ways to strengthen your trust bank:

Keep Promises: Whether it's a small commitment or a major promise, following through is essential. Each time you honor your word, you build credibility and confidence.

Communicate Openly: Transparency nurtures trust. Sharing your thoughts, feelings, and concerns fosters an environment where both partners feel safe and valued.

Be Present: Consistent presence—emotionally and physically—creates a sense of security. Being there for your partner during tough times is a powerful deposit into your trust bank.

Practice Accountability: Acknowledge your mistakes and take responsibility. This not only repairs trust when it's been compromised but also reinforces the idea that both partners are committed to growth.

Show Appreciation: Regularly expressing gratitude and affection can strengthen the emotional bond, making each deposit feel significant and meaningful.

The Long Game

Building a robust trust bank isn't an overnight endeavor; it requires patience and ongoing effort. Relationships inevitably face challenges, and occasional withdrawals are natural. However, consistent deposits can mitigate the effects of these setbacks. It's essential to remember that trust can be rebuilt, but it takes time and commitment to restore a healthy balance.

When both partners understand and actively engage in this trust bank dynamic, they cultivate a relationship rich in reliability and consistency. The result is a deep-seated trust that not only withstands the tests of time but flourishes in the warmth of unwavering support.

In the end, trust is not just about grand gestures but about the everyday acts that affirm commitment and love. By investing consistently in your trust bank, you create a lasting bond, transforming your relationship into a sanctuary of trust where love can thrive.

The Role of Transparency in Fostering Connection

Transparency acts as a vital thread that weaves trust, understanding, and intimacy together. Sharing feelings, fears, and intentions openly is not merely a choice; it's a necessity for nurturing a deep and meaningful connection.

Building Trust Through Openness

When partners practice transparency, they create an environment where vulnerability is welcomed. This openness fosters trust, as each person feels secure enough to express their true selves without fear of judgment. By sharing feelings—whether joyful or painful—partners validate each other's experiences, reinforcing the bond between them. This shared vulnerability not only deepens emotional intimacy but also cultivates a sense of safety, encouraging both individuals to be authentic.

Understanding Fears and Concerns

Every person carries fears and insecurities that can influence their behavior and reactions. When these feelings are shared openly, it allows for greater empathy and understanding. Instead of making assumptions or jumping to conclusions, partners can address concerns together. For example, if one partner fears abandonment, discussing this fear openly can help the other understand the need for reassurance and support, paving the way for a more compassionate response.

Clarifying Intentions

Transparency also extends to intentions. When partners openly communicate their goals and desires, it minimizes misunderstandings and aligns their paths. For instance, discussing long-term aspirations—be it career ambitions, family planning, or personal growth—ensures that both partners are on the same page, working toward a shared vision for the future. This clarity can prevent resentment and confusion, making the relationship stronger and more cohesive.

Creating a Safe Space for Dialogue

Openly sharing feelings, fears, and intentions requires creating a safe space for dialogue. This involves active listening, where each partner feels heard and valued. It's essential to approach conversations with empathy, patience, and a willingness to understand one another's perspectives. When partners commit to this practice, they cultivate an atmosphere of respect and care, where honesty thrives.

The Transformative Power of Transparency

Ultimately, transparency transforms relationships. It turns moments of uncertainty into opportunities for growth, allowing partners to navigate challenges together. By fostering open communication, couples can strengthen their emotional connection, resolve conflicts more effectively, and deepen their love.

In summary, the importance of transparency in sharing feelings, fears, and intentions cannot be overstated. It is the bedrock of trust and intimacy, enabling partners to build a resilient and fulfilling relationship. By embracing openness, couples not only enrich their connection but also embark on a journey of mutual growth and understanding, creating a partnership that stands the test of time.

Rebuilding Trust

Trust, once fractured, can feel daunting to restore, but it is possible with commitment, transparency, and time. Rebuilding trust is a journey that requires both partners to actively participate in the recovery process. Here's a guide to navigating this delicate path.

Steps for Recovery

Acknowledge the Breach: The first step in rebuilding trust is recognizing that a breach has occurred. This requires both partners to confront the issue honestly. The partner who has violated trust must accept responsibility for their actions, acknowledging how these actions affected their partner and the relationship. This acknowledgment sets the stage for meaningful dialogue and understanding.

Apologize Sincerely: A heartfelt apology is essential. It should express genuine remorse and understanding of the pain caused. This isn't just about saying "I'm sorry"; it involves taking ownership of the actions that led to the breach and showing empathy towards the hurt partner's feelings. A sincere apology can begin to heal the emotional wounds and demonstrate a commitment to change.

Create a Plan for Change: Once the breach has been acknowledged and an apology made, it's crucial to develop a plan for change. This involves setting clear expectations and actions to prevent future breaches. Both partners should discuss what changes need to happen to rebuild trust and ensure that both feel secure moving forward. This might include establishing new boundaries, improving communication, or seeking external support, such as counseling.

The Role of Time in Healing Wounds

Rebuilding trust is not an instantaneous process; it requires time. Healing from a breach of trust involves several key aspects:

Patience: Both partners need to be patient with each other and with the process. The partner who was hurt may need time to process their feelings and rebuild their confidence in the relationship. Likewise, the partner who caused the breach must be patient as trust is gradually restored.

Consistency: Over time, consistent actions aligned with the promises made during the recovery process reinforce trust. It's essential for the partner seeking forgiveness to demonstrate reliability through their actions. Each positive interaction acts as a deposit into the trust bank, slowly rebuilding the balance.

Reassurance: Providing reassurance is vital during the healing phase. The partner who has been hurt may experience moments of doubt and insecurity. Regular affirmations of commitment, love, and understanding can help alleviate these feelings and reinforce the idea that the relationship is worth nurturing.

Reflection: Time also allows for reflection. Both partners can take a step back to understand their emotions, motivations, and behaviors. This reflective practice can lead to personal growth and a deeper understanding of each other, strengthening the relationship as a whole.

In conclusion, while rebuilding trust is challenging, it is achievable through acknowledgment, sincere apologies, and a commitment to change. Time plays a crucial role in healing wounds, allowing both partners to process their feelings, rebuild confidence, and create a stronger foundation for their relationship. With patience and dedication, love can emerge renewed, enriched by the journey of recovery.

5. Moments that Matter: Quality Time
 - "In shared moments, we weave the fabric of our love."

In the fabric of love, quality time weaves the threads that hold relationships together, creating vibrant patterns of connection and intimacy. It is during these moments—unhurried and genuine—that partners deepen their understanding of one another, nurture their emotional bonds, and cultivate a sense of belonging. Quality time is not merely about being together; it's about being present, engaged, and open to shared experiences that enrich the heart.

Imagine a cozy evening where the world outside fades away, and it's just you and your partner, savoring laughter over a home-cooked meal or embarking on a spontaneous adventure. These shared moments, however simple, form the foundation of your relationship. They allow you to communicate not just through words, but through shared glances, laughter, and the comfort of silence. Each experience becomes a cherished memory, a touchstone that you can revisit in your minds and hearts.

When partners invest in quality time, they create an environment where vulnerability can thrive. It's in these intimate settings that fears can be shared, dreams can be nurtured, and love can flourish. By prioritizing these moments, couples demonstrate that they value each other's presence, fostering a profound sense of trust and security. This is where emotional bonds are strengthened, as partners learn to navigate life together, embracing both the joys and the challenges that come their way.

In a world filled with distractions, carving out time for each other can feel daunting, yet it is precisely this effort that speaks volumes about your commitment. Quality time is an invitation to slow down, to savor the magic of your connection, and to invest in the ongoing journey of love. As we explore this essential aspect of relationships, let us delve into the myriad ways shared experiences can transform not just your partnership, but your lives as a whole.

The Heart of Chennai: A Journey of Quality Time

In the bustling city of Chennai, where the vibrant chaos of life intertwines with the soothing sounds of the sea, lived a couple, Aarav and Meera. Their love story began like a beautiful melody, resonating with laughter and shared dreams. Yet, as the demands of work and daily responsibilities consumed them, the music began to fade.

Aarav, a dedicated software engineer, often found himself lost in a whirlwind of deadlines and meetings. Meera, a passionate graphic designer, was equally swept away by her own projects. They would exchange brief smiles over hurried breakfasts, and by the time evening arrived, exhaustion would dictate their evenings. TV shows and smartphones became their companions, while meaningful conversations and shared experiences were relegated to the background.

As the months passed, an invisible chasm began to form between them. They realized they were living under the same roof, yet their hearts felt miles apart. It was a Saturday morning when the weight of their disconnect hit them. Aarav glanced at Meera, who sat lost in her phone, her eyes devoid of the spark that once captivated him. "What are we doing?" he finally asked, a hint of frustration in his voice.

Meera sighed, "I don't know, Aarav. We're always so busy. I miss us."

That moment of honesty cracked open the door to a realization they had both avoided: they were missing the essence of their relationship—quality time. They longed for shared laughter, spontaneous adventures, and quiet moments that made them feel alive together.

Determined to change the course of their relationship, they made a pact to prioritize their time together. They started small, scheduling a weekly "date night" where they would explore the city's hidden gems. One Friday, they ventured to a quaint café in Mylapore, where the aroma of freshly brewed filter coffee mingled with the warmth of the setting sun. They shared stories over steaming cups, rediscovering the magic in each other's laughter.

As weeks turned into months, their commitment to quality time transformed their lives. They took long walks along Marina Beach, feeling the gentle breeze against their skin, and engaged in heart-to-heart conversations that flowed like the waves. They experimented with cooking new dishes together, turning the kitchen into a playground of flavors and laughter. Every shared experience, no matter how small, reignited the spark of their love.

One evening, while watching the sunset from the terrace, Aarav turned to Meera, his heart full. "Do you remember when we used to dream about traveling together?" he asked.

Meera smiled, her eyes sparkling. "Yes! Let's make that happen."

Inspired, they began planning weekend getaways, exploring nearby hill stations and historical towns. Each adventure deepened their bond, filling their lives with memories that would last a lifetime.

By the time their anniversary approached, Aarav and Meera had transformed their relationship from a routine into a beautiful journey of connection. They realized that the simple act of prioritizing time together had rekindled the love they thought they had lost.

On the night of their anniversary, Aarav surprised Meera with a heartfelt gift: a scrapbook filled with photographs from their adventures, accompanied by handwritten notes reflecting their shared experiences. As they flipped through the pages, tears of joy filled Meera's eyes.

"This is what I cherish most," Aarav said softly. "It's not just about the big moments; it's about every little one we've created together."

In that embrace, under the twinkling stars of Chennai, Aarav and Meera understood the profound truth about love: it thrives in the moments we choose to share, transforming the ordinary into the extraordinary. Their journey toward quality time had woven their hearts together more tightly than ever, reminding them that love is not just about being together; it's about truly being present.

Research consistently shows that couples who prioritize quality time together experience stronger emotional bonds and greater relationship satisfaction. Here are some key findings:

Enhanced Communication: Studies indicate that couples who spend quality time together tend to communicate more effectively. Engaging in shared activities fosters openness, allowing partners to express their thoughts and feelings, which strengthens their emotional connection.

Increased Relationship Satisfaction: Research published in journals like Journal of Marriage and Family highlights that couples who regularly engage in quality time report higher levels of relationship satisfaction. This is often linked to the creation of shared memories and experiences that reinforce their bond.

Stress Reduction: Quality time can act as a buffer against stress. Couples who prioritize time together often report feeling more supported, which can lead to lower stress levels. A study in The Journal of Family Psychology found that couples who spend time together engage in healthier coping strategies when faced with life's challenges.

Improved Conflict Resolution: Spending quality time together can enhance couples' ability to resolve conflicts. Research suggests that partners who engage in shared experiences are more likely to approach disagreements with empathy and understanding, leading to more constructive resolutions.

Boosted Intimacy: According to a study published in The Archives of Romantic Behavior, couples who prioritize quality time together experience higher levels of intimacy, both emotional and physical. This is often due to the deeper connection formed through shared experiences.

Long-term Relationship Success: Longitudinal studies indicate that couples who regularly invest in quality time together are more likely to maintain their relationships over time. A study by the National Institute of Health found that couples who engage in shared activities, such as date nights or hobbies, report stronger commitment and reduced likelihood of separation.

Development of Shared Goals: Couples who spend quality time together often find themselves aligning on life goals and values. Research has shown that shared experiences lead to discussions about future aspirations, which fosters a sense of partnership and collaboration.

In conclusion, prioritizing quality time is not just about enjoying fun moments; it plays a crucial role in enhancing communication, satisfaction, intimacy, and long-term success in relationships. The evidence supports the idea that making time for each other is one of the most impactful investments a couple can make in their love story.

Ideas for Quality Time

Weekly Date Nights: Schedule a regular night each week dedicated to each other—dinner at a favorite restaurant, a movie night at home, or exploring a new part of the city.

Shared Hobbies: Take up a hobby together, like cooking, painting, or hiking. Engaging in a common interest can deepen your connection.

Nature Walks: Spend time outdoors by going for walks or hikes. Nature can provide a peaceful backdrop for meaningful conversations.

Game Nights: Organize a game night with board games or video games that you both enjoy. It's a fun way to relax and bond.

Volunteer Together: Find a cause you both care about and volunteer. Working together for a common purpose can strengthen your bond.

Travel Adventures: Plan weekend getaways or day trips to explore new places. Traveling together creates lasting memories.

Cooking Together: Prepare a meal together, trying out new recipes or cuisines. Cooking can be a creative and collaborative experience.

Attend Workshops: Sign up for workshops or classes that interest you both, like dance, photography, or pottery.

Necessity of Maintaining Friendship and Personal Interests

Maintaining a strong friendship within a romantic relationship is essential for long-term happiness. It fosters open communication, trust, and support. Here's why it matters:

Emotional Support: Friends provide a safety net during tough times, and this support is vital in a romantic relationship.

Shared Experiences: A strong friendship allows for shared laughter and joy, which enhances emotional intimacy.

Personal Growth: Encouraging each other's interests fosters individual growth, making both partners more fulfilled.

Tips for Scheduling Quality Time and Individual Pursuits

Set Boundaries: Designate specific times for quality time, ensuring that both partners commit to these moments without distractions.

Use a Shared Calendar: Utilize a digital calendar to mark quality time and individual pursuits. This helps in visualizing schedules and avoiding conflicts.

Prioritize: Identify what's most important to both of you and make those activities a priority. Don't hesitate to say no to less meaningful commitments.

Alternate Responsibilities: If planning date nights feels overwhelming, take turns organizing them. This allows both partners to contribute equally.

Schedule "Me Time": Ensure that each person has time for personal interests or relaxation. This can be a few hours each week dedicated to pursuing hobbies or self-care.

Combine Activities: Find ways to blend quality time with personal pursuits. For instance, if one partner enjoys reading, consider a cozy reading session together, discussing books afterward.

Stay Flexible: Life can be unpredictable. Be open to adjusting schedules as needed while keeping quality time and personal interests a priority.

Regular Check-Ins: Schedule regular discussions to assess how both partners feel about the time spent together and apart. Adjust plans as needed to maintain balance.

By intentionally prioritizing both quality time together and individual pursuits, couples can foster a deeper emotional connection while also supporting personal growth, ultimately leading to a healthier and more fulfilling relationship.

Embracing the Journey of Quality Time

As we conclude this chapter on quality time, let's take a moment to reflect on the profound impact these shared experiences can have on our relationships. Life may pull us in a thousand different directions, but it is the time we carve out for one another that serves as the heartbeat of love. When we prioritize these moments, we ignite the spark that fuels our connection, nurturing the bonds that make our journey together not just fulfilling, but truly extraordinary.

Imagine the laughter shared over a game night, the warmth of cooking together, or the quiet intimacy of a stroll under the stars. These are the treasures that form the foundation of a lasting relationship—memories that will sustain you through life's ebbs and flows. By committing to this journey, you're not just enhancing your love; you're creating a beautiful narrative that will unfold with every moment spent together.

So, as you move forward, embrace the adventure of quality time. Discover the joy in each shared experience, and allow your relationship to flourish in unexpected ways. Remember, every moment counts, and every small effort you make contributes to the bigger picture of your love story.

Stay curious, stay engaged, and let your hearts guide you toward new horizons. The path of love is vibrant and ever-evolving, inviting you to explore deeper connections and richer experiences. So, step boldly into the next chapter of your journey together—there are countless joys yet to be uncovered.

Let the excitement of what's to come propel you forward, as you cultivate not just a relationship, but a lifelong friendship filled with love, laughter, and shared dreams. Your journey together is just beginning, and the best is yet to come!

6. The Power of Appreciation

- "Gratitude transforms ordinary days into extraordinary memories."

Appreciation serves as a vital thread that weaves partners closer together. The Law of Appreciation asserts that recognizing and valuing each other's efforts, qualities, and presence not only nurtures a relationship but also fosters deeper intimacy and connection. When partners express appreciation, they validate one another's worth, leading to increased relationship satisfaction and emotional security.

The Power of Appreciation

At its core, appreciation is an acknowledgment of the positive attributes and actions of a partner. It can be as simple as saying "thank you" for daily contributions or recognizing larger sacrifices made for the relationship. This acknowledgment does wonders: it creates a positive feedback loop where both partners feel valued and motivated to continue investing in one another.

Research shows that couples who regularly express appreciation experience higher levels of happiness and satisfaction. When partners feel appreciated, they are more likely to reciprocate with kindness and support, fostering a nurturing environment. This creates a safe space for love to flourish, where both individuals feel seen, heard, and cherished.

Love Languages and Appreciation

Appreciation prominently falls within the realm of Words of Affirmation. For individuals who resonate with this love language, verbal acknowledgments of love and gratitude can be incredibly powerful. A sincere compliment or heartfelt note can brighten their day and deepen their emotional bond with their partner.

However, appreciation can also be intertwined with other love languages. For instance, Acts of Service can be seen as a form of appreciation when one partner goes out of their way to make the other's life easier. Similarly, spending Quality Time together can be enriched through shared experiences of expressing gratitude, enhancing both the time spent together and the connection felt.

Cultivating a Culture of Appreciation

To integrate the Law of Appreciation into your relationship, consider the following practices:

Daily Gratitude: Make it a habit to express one thing you appreciate about your partner each day. This simple practice can significantly shift the focus from what's lacking to what's abundant in your relationship.

Personalized Appreciation: Understand your partner's love language and tailor your expressions of appreciation accordingly. This could mean writing a note, planning a special date, or simply taking the time to listen and engage fully.

Celebrate Small Wins: Acknowledge not just the big milestones but also the everyday actions and efforts that contribute to your relationship. Celebrating these small victories fosters an atmosphere of mutual respect and admiration.

Express Authenticity: Ensure that your appreciation is genuine and specific. Instead of vague compliments, pinpoint particular actions or qualities you love about your partner. This not only feels more meaningful but also shows that you truly notice and value them.

In summary, the Law of Appreciation is a powerful catalyst in love relationships. By fostering a culture of gratitude and understanding each other's love languages, couples can deepen their connection and enhance their relationship satisfaction. In love, it's the little things—appreciation, acknowledgment, and heartfelt gratitude—that make the journey all the more beautiful.

A Story of Appreciation: Rishi and Ananya in Kolkata

In the vibrant heart of Kolkata, where the air was filled with the aroma of street food and the sounds of bustling life, lived a couple named Rishi and Ananya. Their love story blossomed like the blooming lotuses in the tranquil waters of the city's many lakes. They had been together for five years, navigating the ups and downs of life hand in hand.

Rishi, a passionate photographer, often wandered the streets of Kolkata, capturing its essence through his lens. Ananya, an aspiring writer, found inspiration in the tales of the city, often scribbling notes in her journal while sipping tea at their favorite café, College Street. Despite their shared love for art and culture, they had recently found themselves drifting apart, consumed by the demands of their busy lives.

One rainy afternoon, as the monsoon clouds darkened the sky, Rishi returned home drenched and weary. He felt a familiar ache in his heart—not for the rain, but for the connection he felt slipping away from Ananya. She was seated at their dining table, surrounded by a mountain of crumpled papers, struggling with her latest story.

"Hey, you! Look at you," Rishi said with a teasing smile, hoping to lighten the mood. But Ananya barely glanced up, lost in her thoughts.

That night, after a quiet dinner, Rishi felt compelled to bridge the distance between them. He remembered the Law of Appreciation, the importance of recognizing and valuing each other. He took a deep breath, recalling the many little things he adored about Ananya.

"Ananya," he began softly, "can I tell you something?"

She looked up, curious.

"I love how you see the world. Your words bring life to the stories that fill this city. I've seen you pour your heart into every line you write. It's beautiful." His voice was sincere, filled with warmth.

Ananya's eyes softened. "Thank you, Rishi. But I often feel like I'm not good enough."

"Are you kidding?" Rishi chuckled lightly. "Your writing has a way of capturing emotions that I could never convey through my photographs. Remember that piece you wrote about the old man at the park? It made me cry."

Her heart swelled with gratitude, and for the first time in weeks, Ananya smiled genuinely. "I didn't think anyone noticed."

"Of course, I notice! And I appreciate you. You bring joy to my life every day." He took her hands in his, grounding them both in the moment.

Encouraged by his words, Ananya decided to reciprocate. "You know, Rishi, your photographs inspire me. Every time I see you work, it reminds me of the beauty that exists around us. You see stories in the ordinary, and that's a gift."

As they spoke, the air between them shifted. The connection they had once felt began to rekindle. They shared stories, reminiscing about their early days together—the spontaneous trips to Howrah Bridge and their quiet evenings at the Victoria Memorial, laughing and dreaming.

In the days that followed, they continued this practice of appreciation. Each morning, before leaving for their respective work, they took a moment to express gratitude. "Thank you for making my coffee just right," Ananya would say. "I love how you make me laugh, even on tough days," Rishi would reply.

Slowly but surely, the love they shared flourished once again. Their home transformed into a haven of encouragement, where each supported the other's dreams. Ananya completed her writing projects with renewed enthusiasm, and Rishi found himself capturing even more extraordinary moments through his lens, inspired by Ananya's passion.

One evening, as the sun set over the Hooghly River, they sat side by side, watching the boats drift by. Ananya rested her head on Rishi's shoulder, a contented sigh escaping her lips.

"Thank you for reminding me how wonderful I am," she whispered.

"Thank you for being you," Rishi replied, kissing the top of her head.

In the heart of Kolkata, amidst the vibrant life and chaos, Rishi and Ananya discovered that appreciation was the key to reigniting their love. It was the little things—a kind word, a heartfelt gesture, a moment of acknowledgment—that strengthened their bond and filled their lives with joy. And as they walked hand in hand through the city they adored, they knew their love story was far from over; it was just beginning anew, richer and more profound than ever.

Here are some practical ways to show appreciation through daily affirmations, reminders for gratitude, and thoughtful acts of kindness:

Daily Affirmations

Morning Messages: Start each day by sending a sweet text or leaving a note that expresses what you appreciate about your partner.

Compliment of the Day: Make it a routine to give one genuine compliment every day. Focus on different aspects like appearance, effort, or character.

Gratitude Jar: Create a jar where you both drop in notes throughout the week with things you appreciate about each other. Read them together at the end of the week.

Setting Reminders to Express Gratitude

Calendar Alerts: Set daily or weekly reminders on your phone to prompt you to express appreciation. It could be as simple as sending a text or verbally acknowledging your partner.

Sticky Notes: Place sticky notes in visible places (like the bathroom mirror or refrigerator) with reminders to appreciate your partner, inspiring spontaneous expressions of gratitude.

Gratitude App: Use an app designed for gratitude practice, where you can log daily appreciations and set reminders for sharing them with your partner.

Acts of Kindness and Thoughtful Gestures

Leave a Sweet Note: Tuck a note into your partner's bag or lunch, expressing something you love about them or a simple "I appreciate you."

Small Surprises: Bring home their favorite treat or snack unexpectedly. It shows you're thinking of them.

Cook a Meal: Prepare a meal they love, or surprise them with breakfast in bed on a weekend.

Help with Tasks: Take on a chore your partner dislikes, like doing the dishes or laundry, to lighten their load.

Create a Relaxation Space: Set up a cozy area at home for them to unwind, complete with their favorite book, snacks, and a comfy blanket.

Complimentary Gesture: Offer a massage after a long day, showing you care about their well-being.

Plan a Surprise Date: Organize a spontaneous outing, like a picnic in the park or a visit to a local event, to spend quality time together.

Create a Memory: Frame a photo of a special moment or create a small scrapbook of your favorite memories together, highlighting how much those times mean to you.

By integrating these daily affirmations, reminders, and thoughtful gestures into your routine, you can cultivate a deeper sense of appreciation in your relationship and strengthen your bond.

Impact of Consistent Appreciation on Emotional Connection

Consistent appreciation plays a crucial role in enhancing emotional connection in relationships. When partners regularly acknowledge and value each other, it fosters an environment of trust, safety, and mutual respect. This positive reinforcement not only strengthens the bond but also deepens intimacy, making each partner feel seen, heard, and valued.

Benefits of Consistent Appreciation

Increased Trust: Regular expressions of appreciation help build trust between partners. When each person feels valued, they are more likely to be open and vulnerable, sharing their thoughts and feelings without fear of judgment.

Strengthened Emotional Bond: Appreciation enhances feelings of closeness and connection. It reminds partners of their shared values and the reasons they came together, reinforcing their emotional ties.

Boosted Self-Esteem: Knowing that your partner appreciates you can significantly boost self-esteem and confidence. This, in turn, leads to a more positive outlook on the relationship and oneself.

Improved Communication: When appreciation is a consistent practice, partners are more likely to communicate openly. They feel encouraged to express their needs and desires, leading to healthier discussions.

Counteracting Negativity

In any relationship, negativity can creep in due to stress, misunderstandings, or external pressures. However, consistent appreciation serves as a powerful antidote to negativity for several reasons:

Shifting Focus: When appreciation becomes a regular part of the relationship, it shifts the focus from what's lacking or problematic to what's positive and fulfilling. This shift can help partners see their relationship through a more optimistic lens.

Creating a Positive Cycle: Regularly expressing gratitude fosters a positive feedback loop. When one partner feels appreciated, they are more likely to reciprocate, creating a cycle of positivity that can counteract negative feelings or behaviors.

Reducing Conflict: Appreciation can diffuse tension during conflicts. When partners remind each other of their strengths and the good aspects of their relationship, it can soften criticisms and reduce defensiveness.

Building Resilience: Couples who practice consistent appreciation are better equipped to handle challenges. The strong emotional connection they've built enables them to weather storms together, knowing they can rely on each other's support.

Enhancing Forgiveness: Appreciation can make it easier to forgive mistakes or misunderstandings. When partners regularly express gratitude, it creates a foundation of goodwill that makes it easier to overlook minor grievances.

Consistent appreciation is a powerful tool in nurturing emotional connection and counteracting negativity in relationships. By fostering a culture of gratitude, partners can enhance their bond, build resilience, and create a positive environment where love can thrive. When both individuals feel valued and appreciated, they are more likely to contribute positively to the relationship, leading to lasting happiness and fulfillment.

Embracing the Journey of Love Through Appreciation

As we conclude this chapter on the Law of Appreciation in love relationships, let us take a moment to reflect on the profound impact that gratitude and acknowledgment can have on our connections. In a world often filled with distractions and challenges, taking the time to appreciate one another becomes a powerful act of love.

By cultivating consistent appreciation, we not only strengthen our emotional bonds but also create a nurturing space where love can thrive. Each word of gratitude, every thoughtful gesture, and all moments of shared joy contribute to the beautiful tapestry of our relationships. They remind us that love is not just a feeling but a practice—one that requires attention, intention, and heartfelt connection.

As you embark on your own journey of discovering love, may you find joy in the little things, courage in vulnerability, and strength in the appreciation you offer and receive. Embrace the power of gratitude as a guiding light, illuminating the path to deeper intimacy and understanding.

Wishing you all the best on this journey—may your hearts be open, your connections be rich, and your love be ever-growing. Here's to a life filled with appreciation, love, and endless possibilities!

7. The Gift of Support

 - "In love, we rise together, hand in hand through challenges."

Imagine love as a vessel navigating the unpredictable seas of existence. In this journey, the waves of doubt, stress, and uncertainty can toss even the sturdiest of ships. Yet, when partners commit to being each other's emotional support, they become the lighthouse guiding one another home. This mutual support is not just a refuge; it is a celebration of shared strength, where vulnerabilities are embraced and fears are confronted together.

Being each other's anchor means creating a safe space for expression, where words and feelings flow freely without judgment. It's in those moments of vulnerability that true intimacy flourishes. When one partner faces challenges, the other offers unwavering encouragement, reminding them that they are not alone. This bond nurtures resilience, allowing both partners to grow, evolve, and face life's obstacles hand in hand.

Moreover, emotional support fosters a deep sense of belonging. It's the knowledge that, no matter the circumstances, there is someone who believes in you wholeheartedly. This belief nurtures confidence and empowers individuals to chase their dreams and confront their fears, knowing they have a partner cheering them on.

In relationships where support is prioritized, love transforms into a powerful force, capable of overcoming any adversity. Each act of encouragement, each moment of understanding, builds a

foundation that can withstand the test of time. Together, partners create a legacy of resilience, compassion, and unwavering support—a true testament to the beauty of love.

As we delve into the heart of this chapter, let us explore the myriad ways we can embody the Law of Support in our relationships, and discover how being each other's emotional anchors can elevate our love to new heights.

A Love Anchored in Hyderabad

In the bustling heart of Hyderabad, where the rich aroma of biryani wafted through the streets and the historic grandeur of the Charminar stood as a sentinel of time, lived two souls destined to find each other: Amina and Rohan.

Amina was a spirited artist, known for her vibrant paintings that captured the essence of her beloved city. Her studio was a kaleidoscope of colors, filled with canvases depicting the lively markets, serene lakes, and bustling streets of Hyderabad. Despite her talent, she often grappled with self-doubt, questioning whether her art could truly resonate with others.

Rohan, on the other hand, was a diligent software engineer, his days filled with coding and deadlines. He was driven by ambition, yet his heart lay in the stories of his city. He admired Amina from afar, enchanted by her creativity and passion. Though he often masked his admiration with a friendly smile, he felt a magnetic pull towards her.

One day, at an art exhibition, Rohan mustered the courage to approach Amina. As they talked, he felt an instant connection, like two pieces of a puzzle fitting together seamlessly. Amina shared her insecurities about her art, her voice laced with hesitation. Rohan listened intently, his heart aching for her struggles.

"Your art tells stories that words cannot," he said, his eyes sparkling with sincerity. "You have a gift that the world needs to see. I believe in you."

His words ignited a flicker of hope within Amina. In that moment, she realized that support could be transformative, grounding her like the roots of a sturdy banyan tree.

As their friendship blossomed into love, Rohan became Amina's emotional anchor. When self-doubt crept in, he would remind her of the beauty she created. "Let's visit the lake tomorrow," he suggested one evening, pulling her from her worries. "We can sketch together. The tranquility might inspire you."

At Hussain Sagar Lake, with the sun setting in hues of gold and crimson, Amina felt her worries melt away. They sketched the silhouette of the Buddha statue rising from the water, laughter filling the air. Rohan's unwavering support became a canvas for Amina's spirit, allowing her to flourish.

In turn, Amina became Rohan's anchor as he faced challenges at work. When a crucial project faltered, he felt overwhelmed. Late into the night, he confided in her, the weight of his worries heavy on his shoulders. Amina listened, her hand gently resting on his. "You're capable of more than you realize," she whispered, her voice soothing. "Remember how you solved that complex problem last month? You've got this."

With Amina's belief in him, Rohan found renewed strength. He approached his challenges with a fresh perspective, leaning into her unwavering support. Together, they navigated the highs and lows, their bond deepening with each shared moment.

As seasons changed, so did their relationship. They celebrated milestones—Amina's first solo exhibition, where Rohan stood proudly by her side, and Rohan's promotion, where Amina organized a surprise celebration in the vibrant lanes of Banjara Hills. Each triumph was a testament to their commitment to uplift one another.

One evening, as they walked through the streets adorned with twinkling lights, Rohan paused. "Amina," he said, his voice steady, "you've taught me that love isn't just about passion. It's about support, understanding, and being there through it all."

Amina smiled, her heart swelling with affection. "And you've shown me that believing in each other can turn dreams into reality."

In that moment, they realized that their love was not just a beautiful chapter but an unbreakable bond. It was anchored in mutual support, creating a foundation that would carry them through life's unpredictable tides.

As they embraced under the stars, the city around them hummed with life. Their hearts, intertwined, whispered a promise: to always be each other's anchors, come what may.

And in the vibrant city of Hyderabad, their love story became a testament to the power of support, illustrating that together, they could weather any storm.

The Art of Being a Good Listener

In the symphony of human connection, being a good listener is like holding the most important note—essential, resonant, and profoundly impactful. Listening is not merely the act of hearing words; it is an art that fosters understanding, deepens relationships, and creates a safe space for sharing. When we embrace the role of an active listener, we open the door to genuine connection and empathy.

The Importance of Listening

In our fast-paced world, where distractions abound and conversations often race by, the simple act of listening can feel like a rare gift. It conveys respect, shows that we value the speaker's thoughts, and affirms their feelings. When someone knows they are truly heard, it creates a bond of trust and intimacy, allowing them to express themselves more freely.

Techniques for Active Listening

Be Present: Give your full attention to the speaker. Put away distractions—your phone, the television, or any mental to-do lists. Maintain eye contact, nod occasionally, and use body language that reflects your engagement. This physical presence communicates your genuine interest.

Reflective Listening: This technique involves mirroring what the speaker has said, but in your own words. For instance, if someone shares their feelings of stress about work, you might respond, "It sounds like you're feeling overwhelmed with your workload." This not only shows that you're listening but also allows the speaker to clarify their thoughts and feelings.

Validation: Acknowledging the speaker's emotions is crucial. Validation involves affirming their feelings without judgment. You might say, "I can see why you'd feel that way; it makes sense given what you're going through." This helps the speaker feel accepted and understood, reinforcing that their emotions are valid.

Ask Open-Ended Questions: Encourage deeper conversation by asking questions that require more than a yes or no answer. Questions like "What was that experience like for you?" or "How did that make you feel?" invite the speaker to share more, enhancing the dialogue.

Summarize and Paraphrase: Occasionally summarizing what the speaker has shared helps reinforce your understanding. For example, "So what you're saying is..." allows you to clarify any misunderstandings and demonstrates that you are genuinely engaged in the conversation.

Empathy: Put yourself in the speaker's shoes. Try to understand their feelings and perspectives. Empathetic listening involves connecting with the emotional undertone of the conversation, which deepens your understanding and strengthens your bond.

The Transformative Power of Listening

When practiced with intention, these techniques can transform conversations into meaningful exchanges. Good listening nurtures relationships, fostering an environment where both partners feel safe to express themselves. It encourages openness and vulnerability, creating a foundation for love and understanding.

In the end, being a good listener is one of the greatest gifts we can offer one another. It tells the other person that they matter, that their thoughts and feelings are valued, and that in this moment, they are not alone. So, let us embrace the art of listening, for in doing so, we weave the threads of connection that hold our relationships together, making them more beautiful and resilient.

Supporting Dreams and Ambitions

In the landscape of a loving relationship, supporting each other's dreams and ambitions is akin to nurturing a flourishing garden. Just as plants require sunlight, water, and care to thrive, so too do our aspirations need encouragement and belief from those we love. When partners commit to uplifting each other's goals, they cultivate a partnership that fosters growth, resilience, and shared joy.

Helping Each Other Set and Achieve Personal Goals

Open Communication: Start by creating an open dialogue about your dreams and ambitions. Share your aspirations, no matter how big or small, and encourage your partner to do the same. This exchange lays the foundation for mutual understanding and support.

Set SMART Goals: Work together to establish Specific, Measurable, Achievable, Relevant, and Time-bound (SMART) goals. This framework not only clarifies what you both want to achieve but also provides a structured path forward. For example, if one partner aims to advance in their career, break down the steps needed to get there, such as networking, acquiring new skills, or seeking mentorship.

Be Each Other's Accountability Partner: Regularly check in on each other's progress. These conversations can serve as motivation, helping both partners stay on track. Celebrate milestones, no matter how small, and discuss any challenges faced along the way. This accountability fosters a sense of teamwork and partnership.

Provide Constructive Feedback: Offer encouragement while also being honest about potential obstacles. Constructive feedback is essential in helping your partner refine their goals and strategies. Approach these conversations with sensitivity, ensuring your partner feels supported and valued.

Encourage Self-Care: Pursuing dreams can be demanding, and it's crucial to prioritize self-care. Encourage each other to take breaks, practice mindfulness, or engage in hobbies. This balance helps maintain motivation and prevents burnout.

Celebrating Each Other's Success

Celebrating achievements is just as vital as the support provided during the journey. When one partner reaches a goal, it's an opportunity for both to bask in the shared joy of success.

Acknowledge Milestones: Take the time to recognize and celebrate each other's accomplishments, whether it's a promotion, completing a project, or achieving a personal goal. Simple gestures like a heartfelt note, a celebratory dinner, or even a weekend getaway can make the moment special.

Create a Culture of Celebration: Make it a tradition to celebrate each other's successes regularly. This could involve setting aside time each month to reflect on accomplishments, big or small, fostering a positive and motivating atmosphere.

Express gratitude: Alongside celebration, express gratitude for each other's support throughout the journey. Acknowledge the role your partner played in your success, reinforcing the idea that you are in this together.

Share Success with Loved Ones: When appropriate, involve friends and family in the celebration. This not only amplifies the joy but also strengthens the bonds of your support network.

In the end, supporting each other's dreams and ambitions transforms a relationship into a powerful partnership. When partners stand side by side, cheering each other on, they create a foundation of love, trust, and resilience. By celebrating successes together, they not only enhance their individual journeys but also deepen their connection, creating a shared narrative of growth and achievement that can last a lifetime.

Conclusion: The Power of Support in Love

As we conclude this chapter on the Law of Support, let us reflect on the profound impact that uplifting one another can have on a relationship. In a world often filled with challenges and uncertainties, the strength of a partnership lies in its ability to nurture dreams and ambitions. When two people commit to being each other's anchors, they create a safe haven where aspirations can flourish.

Support is not merely a series of actions; it is a deep-rooted belief in one another's potential. It is the gentle nudge that encourages growth, the warm embrace during moments of doubt, and the joyous celebration of each success. Together, partners can navigate life's complexities, transforming obstacles into stepping stones.

By openly sharing dreams and setting goals, you forge a path that is uniquely yours, marked by collaboration and mutual encouragement. The commitment to support each other not only strengthens your bond but also enhances your individual journeys, allowing both partners to shine brightly.

Remember, every small act of support adds up. Whether through kind words, thoughtful gestures, or shared celebrations, each moment strengthens the tapestry of your relationship. As you continue to explore your dreams and ambitions, cherish the incredible power of being each other's biggest fans.

In the end, it is this unwavering support that transforms a relationship into a beautiful partnership—one where love, dreams, and ambitions intertwine, creating a legacy of resilience and joy. Embrace this journey together, and watch as your love blossoms in ways you never imagined.

8. The Art of Compromise
- "In the dance of love, we step lightly for each other."

The Necessity of Compromise

At its core, compromise is the art of finding common ground. In any relationship, differences are inevitable—whether they stem from personality traits, backgrounds, or life experiences. These differences can lead to conflicts, but they can also provide opportunities for growth. Compromise allows partners to step into each other's shoes, recognizing that love is not merely about personal fulfillment but about mutual support and collaboration.

Why Compromise is Vital for Relationship Harmony

Builds Trust and Respect: When partners are willing to meet halfway, it signals a deep respect for one another's feelings and opinions. This mutual understanding fosters trust, reinforcing the bond that holds the relationship together.

Encourages Open Communication: The process of compromise requires honest dialogue. Couples learn to express their needs and concerns while also being receptive to their partner's viewpoint. This open line of communication is essential for resolving conflicts and preventing misunderstandings.

Promotes Emotional Intimacy: As partners navigate their differences, they share their vulnerabilities. This sharing deepens emotional intimacy, as each person learns more about the other's values and aspirations. Such vulnerability can create a stronger emotional connection.

Enhances Problem-Solving Skills: Compromise is a practical exercise in problem-solving. It encourages couples to think creatively, seek solutions together, and develop strategies that work for both parties. This collaborative approach can strengthen the relationship's foundation.

Fosters Resilience: Relationships are tested by challenges, and the ability to compromise equips couples with resilience. When partners learn to adapt and adjust to each other's needs, they become better equipped to face future obstacles together.

Creates a Balanced Partnership: A healthy relationship thrives on balance. Compromise ensures that both partners feel valued and heard, preventing feelings of resentment or imbalance. It nurtures a sense of equality, where both individuals contribute to the relationship's dynamics.

Nurtures Long-Term Harmony: Ultimately, the willingness to compromise is essential for the longevity of a relationship. It transforms potential conflicts into opportunities for growth and connection, laying the groundwork for a lasting partnership.

the law of compromise is not merely a strategy for conflict resolution; it is a fundamental principle that fosters love, understanding, and harmony in relationships. By embracing compromise, couples can navigate the complexities of their differences, celebrating their uniqueness while cultivating a shared journey of love. In this delicate dance of give and take, love flourishes, deepening the bond that unites two souls.

A Story of Compromise: Kavya and Viren in Ahmedabad

In the vibrant city of Ahmedabad, where the aroma of street food mingles with the sounds of bustling markets, lived a couple named Kavya and Viren. They were both in their late twenties, and their lives were a beautiful blend of tradition and modernity. Kavya was a passionate graphic designer, known for her creativity and colourful spirit, while Viren was a pragmatic software engineer, grounded and detail-oriented.

Their love story began during a Navratri festival, where the two found themselves dancing in sync amidst the swirling colours and joyous laughter. As their relationship blossomed, they often reveled in the things that made them different. However, as time went on, those very differences began to surface as challenges.

One evening, while sipping chai at their favorite tea stall, Kavya excitedly shared her dream of opening a design studio. "Viren, just imagine! A space where creativity flows and we can host workshops!" Her eyes sparkled with enthusiasm.

Viren, however, had practical concerns. "Kavya, starting a business is risky. What about our savings? We need stability first," he replied, a hint of worry in his voice.

This conversation sparked a series of disagreements. Kavya felt stifled by Viren's caution, while Viren feared the unpredictability of Kavya's ambitions. Each discussion seemed to push them further apart, creating an undercurrent of tension that threatened their love.

One rainy evening, after a particularly heated argument about finances, Kavya took a long walk along the Sabarmati Riverfront. The rain mirrored her feelings—heavy and tumultuous. As she watched the water flow, she realized that relationships, like rivers, required both direction and adaptability.

That night, as they sat in silence, Kavya decided to approach the situation differently. "Viren," she began softly, "I understand your concerns. But can we find a middle ground? What if we start small? I could take on freelance projects while we save up?"

Viren looked at her, surprised by her openness. "I hadn't thought of that. I just want to ensure we're secure," he replied, his voice calming. "If it means a compromise, I'm willing to support you. Let's create a budget and a plan."

From that moment, their discussions shifted from confrontation to collaboration. They spent evenings mapping out Kavya's business idea while balancing their finances. They even turned their living room into a brainstorming hub, covered in sketches, post-it notes, and plans.

With each step, they not only strengthened Kavya's dream but also deepened their connection. Kavya learned to appreciate Viren's practicality, understanding that it came from a place of love and concern for their future. Viren, in turn, admired Kavya's passion and creativity, realizing that taking calculated risks could lead to fulfillment.

Months passed, and Kavya launched her first small project—a graphic design workshop in their community. The turnout was overwhelming, filled with young artists eager to learn. Viren was there, supporting her every step of the way, and together they celebrated the success of the event.

Their journey was not without its bumps, but through each challenge, they remembered the importance of compromise.

They found joy in creating a life that blended Kavya's dreams and Viren's practicality. The more they communicated, the more they discovered that their differences were not obstacles but opportunities to grow together.

As they walked hand-in-hand along the Sabarmati River one evening, Kavya smiled at Viren. "You know, I couldn't have done this without you," she said, leaning into him.

Viren smiled back, his heart full. "And I've learned that a little compromise can lead to something beautiful. We're building this together."

In the heart of Ahmedabad, Kavya and Viren's love story continued to flourish, a testament to the power of compromise—a reminder that love isn't just about harmony; it's about navigating differences and emerging stronger together.

Finding Common Ground: Steps for Effective Negotiation and Compromise in Disagreements

In any relationship, disagreements are a natural part of life. However, finding common ground can transform these conflicts into opportunities for growth and understanding. Here's a guide to effective negotiation and compromise during disagreements.

Understanding Common Ground

Common ground refers to shared interests, goals, or values that can serve as a foundation for discussion. It helps both parties feel understood and valued, fostering a cooperative atmosphere rather than a confrontational one.

Understanding Healthy and Unhealthy Compromise

Compromise is often seen as a cornerstone of successful relationships, but not all compromises are created equal. It's important to distinguish between healthy and unhealthy compromises to ensure that both partners feel respected and valued.

Healthy Compromise

Characteristics of Healthy Compromise:

Mutual Respect: Both partners acknowledge each other's feelings, needs, and desires.

Open Communication: Honest dialogue about concerns and preferences takes place.

Balance of Needs: Each person gives and takes equally, leading to a win-win situation.

Shared Responsibility: Both partners feel equally involved in the decision-making process.

Emotional Well-Being: Both individuals feel good about the outcome, even if it involves some level of sacrifice.

Examples of Healthy Compromise:

Agreeing to alternate weekends between visiting family and spending time together.

One partner adjusting their work hours to accommodate the other's schedule without feeling resentful.

Unhealthy Compromise

Characteristics of Unhealthy Compromise:

Resentment: One partner feels they are giving up too much or compromising more than the other.

Lack of Voice: One partner dominates the decision-making process, leaving the other feeling unheard.

Emotional Distress: The compromise leads to feelings of frustration, anger, or sadness rather than satisfaction.

One-Sided Sacrifice: One partner consistently sacrifices their needs for the other's comfort or convenience.

Examples of Unhealthy Compromise:

One partner consistently agreeing to plans they dislike just to avoid conflict.

Sacrificing personal goals and aspirations for the sake of the relationship without mutual agreement.

Differentiating Between Sacrifice, Needs, and Finding Balance

Sacrifice:

Sacrifice involves giving up something valuable for the benefit of the other person or the relationship. While sacrifice can be a part of healthy compromise, it should not be one-sided.

Healthy sacrifice occurs when both partners recognize and appreciate the effort made, leading to a strengthened bond.

Example: One partner staying late at work occasionally to support the other during a busy period.

Needs:

Needs refer to the fundamental requirements each person has for emotional well-being, security, and happiness. These can include love, respect, and personal space.

Healthy compromise addresses both partners' needs, ensuring that no one feels neglected or unimportant.

Example: One partner needing quality time together while the other needs personal space, leading to scheduled "couple time" and "me time."

Finding Balance:

Finding balance means ensuring that both partners' needs and desires are met without feeling overwhelmed or taken advantage of. It's about creating a sense of equality in the relationship.

Healthy compromise seeks to achieve this balance by allowing both partners to feel fulfilled and valued.

Example: Agreeing to both take turns choosing activities for date night, ensuring that both partners feel included and appreciated.

Understanding the difference between healthy and unhealthy compromise is crucial for maintaining a strong relationship. By recognizing the roles of sacrifice, needs, and balance, couples can navigate disagreements in a way that fosters mutual respect and understanding. Healthy compromise enhances the relationship, ensuring both partners feel valued and fulfilled, while unhealthy compromise can lead to resentment and emotional distance. Ultimately, the goal is to find a harmonious balance that nurtures both individuals and strengthens their bond.

Embracing the Law of Compromise

As we conclude this chapter on the law of compromise, it's essential to recognize that relationships are not merely about love but also about understanding, collaboration, and growth. Compromise is the bridge that connects differing perspectives, transforming potential conflicts into opportunities for deeper connection.

In a world where individual desires often clash, the ability to meet halfway becomes a powerful tool. It's about finding that delicate balance where both partners feel valued and heard. Healthy compromise encourages open communication, nurtures trust, and fosters a sense of partnership that can weather any storm.

Remember, compromise does not mean surrendering your values or desires; it means embracing a shared journey. It's the art of giving and receiving, of listening and being heard. When both partners are committed to this dance, they create a rhythm that strengthens their bond, making it resilient and enduring.

As you navigate your own relationships, keep in mind that every disagreement carries the potential for growth. Approach conflicts with an open heart and a willingness to understand your partner's perspective. Celebrate the moments of compromise, for they are the stepping stones to harmony and understanding.

In the end, the law of compromise reminds us that love flourishes not in perfection, but in the beautiful, imperfect dance of two unique souls learning to move together. By embracing compromise, you are not only enriching your relationship but also crafting a story of love that is relatable, inspiring, and deeply human. Here's to building a future where love, understanding, and compromise intertwine, creating a life filled with joy and connection.

9. The Beauty of Individuality
 - "Love flourishes in the distinctive fabric of our souls."

The Law of Individuality stands as a vital principle that celebrates the unique essence of each partner. At its core, this law emphasizes the importance of personal identity—not merely as a backdrop to the partnership but as a vibrant, essential thread that enriches the tapestry of love.

Every individual brings a distinct set of experiences, values, dreams, and quirks into a relationship. Embracing these differences fosters a deeper connection and appreciation for one another. When partners honor each other's individuality, they create a safe space for authentic self-expression. This environment nurtures growth, allowing each person to flourish not just as part of a couple, but as whole, complete beings.

Moreover, the Law of Individuality acts as a bulwark against co-dependency, which can insidiously creep into relationships when one partner loses sight of their own identity. In a healthy partnership, each person supports the other's journey, celebrating achievements and providing solace during challenges without losing themselves in the process. This balance of independence and interdependence enhances emotional resilience, encouraging both partners to thrive.

Understanding and honoring individuality means recognizing that love is not about merging into a single entity, but rather about two people choosing to walk alongside each other. It is the appreciation of each other's passions, interests, and quirks that turns a relationship into a vibrant partnership.

In this chapter, we will delve deeper into how the recognition of individuality strengthens bonds, fosters mutual respect, and ultimately cultivates a love that is both enduring and dynamic. By celebrating who we are as individuals, we enrich our relationships, creating a foundation built on authenticity and mutual admiration. As we navigate the complexities of love, let us remember: true connection is not found in losing ourselves, but in the beauty of being wholly, unapologetically ourselves—together.

Sakshi and Manish

In the vibrant heart of Pune, where the old-world charm blends seamlessly with modern aspirations, lived a couple named Sakshi and Manish. They were often seen exploring the city's bustling streets, laughing over cups of steaming chai, or enjoying quiet evenings at their favorite park. Yet, beneath the surface of their joyful relationship lay a powerful understanding of the Law of Individuality, which shaped the very foundation of their love.

Sakshi was a passionate artist, her days filled with splashes of color and the rhythm of her brush against canvas. Manish, on the other hand, was a meticulous engineer, his world governed by precision and logic. At first glance, one might think their differences would create a rift, but instead, they became the cornerstone of their bond.

From the beginning, both Sakshi and Manish cherished their individual passions. Sakshi would often spend weekends at art exhibitions, drawing inspiration from fellow artists, while Manish would dive deep into his engineering projects, relishing the satisfaction of solving complex problems. They never hesitated to share these experiences with each other. Sakshi would bring Manish along to gallery openings, where he would admire her creativity, while she would eagerly listen to his ideas about innovative designs, fascinated by his perspective.

One evening, while discussing their dreams over dinner, Sakshi voiced a longing to host her own art exhibition. The thought made her heart race with excitement, but it also filled her with anxiety. "What if no one likes my work?" she confessed, her voice tinged with doubt. Manish looked at her, his eyes steady and reassuring. "You have to believe in your art, Sakshi. Your individuality is what makes your work special. Let the world see it," he encouraged.

Inspired by Manish's unwavering support, Sakshi poured her heart into her exhibition. She embraced her unique style, allowing her creativity to flow freely. Manish, in turn, took on the role of her biggest cheerleader. He helped her set up the event, using his organizational skills to ensure everything was perfect. His belief in her talent allowed Sakshi to step into the spotlight with confidence.

On the night of the exhibition, surrounded by friends and art enthusiasts, Sakshi watched as people admired her work. Each compliment filled her with joy, but it was Manish's proud smile that truly lit up her heart. He had not only encouraged her to embrace her individuality but had also created a space where she could thrive.

As they celebrated that night, Sakshi realized how their differences had enriched their relationship. Manish's logical approach balanced her creative chaos, while her artistic spirit added color to his structured world. They had learned to appreciate and respect each other's individuality, which deepened their emotional connection and fostered mutual growth.

In the years that followed, this understanding of individuality became their guiding principle. They supported each other through challenges, whether it was Sakshi facing artist block or Manish tackling demanding projects. They shared their successes and failures, always returning to the foundation of their relationship—the belief that both of them were complete individuals.

The Law of Individuality transformed Sakshi and Manish's relationship into a beautiful partnership where both could flourish. Their love story became a testament to the idea that true intimacy does not require losing oneself but rather celebrating who you are. They inspired those around them, showing that when partners honor each other's individuality, they create a love that is not just enduring but also profoundly enriching.

As they walked hand in hand through the streets of Pune, Sakshi and Manish embodied the essence of the Law of Individuality—two unique souls dancing in harmony, creating a life together that was vibrant, authentic, and undeniably beautiful.

Encouraging Personal Growth in Relationships

Personal growth is a vibrant thread that adds depth and richness to the bond shared between partners. Encouraging each other's growth not only nurtures individuality but also strengthens the relationship, fostering a deeper connection and understanding.

Supporting Hobbies and Interests

One of the most beautiful ways to encourage personal growth is by actively supporting each other's hobbies and interests. This means not just tolerating but genuinely engaging in the activities that ignite passion in your partner. Whether it's attending a cooking class together, cheering them on at a sports event, or simply making space for them to indulge in their favorite pastimes, these actions demonstrate love and respect for their individuality.

You might surprise your partner with tickets to a concert of their favorite band, or gift them art supplies for their next creative project. These thoughtful gestures show that you value their interests and are invested in their happiness. Additionally, you could explore new hobbies together, creating shared experiences that enrich both your lives.

Nurturing Friendships

Friendships outside the romantic relationship are equally essential for personal growth. Encourage your partner to maintain connections with friends and family, understanding that these relationships provide a support system that complements your bond. Regularly check in on how they're spending time with friends, and support their plans, whether it's a weekend getaway or a simple coffee catch-up.

Moreover, cultivate an environment where friendships can flourish within the relationship. Invite your partner's friends over, and create opportunities for shared experiences with your own circle. This blend of social networks can enhance your bond while allowing each person to thrive individually.

Communicating Openly

Open communication is the cornerstone of supporting each other's growth. Discuss your dreams, aspirations, and even fears with one another. Encourage each other to set personal goals, whether they're related to career aspirations, health, or creative pursuits. Celebrate achievements, big and small, and offer a listening ear during challenges.

Creating Space for Growth

Make sure both partners have the space to pursue their personal development. This might mean allowing time for solo activities or providing encouragement to take courses or workshops. Recognize that growth can sometimes lead to changes in the relationship dynamic, and approach these shifts with curiosity and openness, rather than fear.

By fostering an environment of support and encouragement, you not only allow each other to grow as individuals but also deepen the connection you share. Personal growth is a journey best taken together, where both partners feel valued, inspired, and free to pursue their passions. In celebrating each other's individuality, you cultivate a love that is resilient, dynamic, and profoundly enriching, transforming your relationship into a beautiful partnership that thrives on mutual respect and admiration.

Balancing Togetherness and Individuality

In the journey of love, finding the right balance between togetherness and individuality is essential for a healthy, fulfilling relationship. While shared experiences create strong bonds, personal time fosters growth and self-discovery.

Striking this balance allows both partners to thrive as individuals while nurturing their connection.

Understanding the Importance of Balance

Togetherness brings joy, intimacy, and shared memories, while individuality promotes self-awareness and personal growth. A relationship that embraces both aspects can withstand challenges and evolve over time. When partners support each other's needs for connection and personal space, they cultivate a healthier, more resilient bond.

Tips for Maintaining a Healthy Balance

Communicate Openly: Regularly discuss your needs and feelings. Share your desire for personal time while expressing the importance of shared activities. Understanding each other's perspectives is key to finding a harmonious balance.

Schedule Shared Activities: Plan regular date nights or shared hobbies to strengthen your bond. These moments of togetherness create cherished memories and provide a foundation for your relationship.

Prioritize Personal Time: Encourage each other to pursue individual interests, whether it's a hobby, exercise, or simply some quiet time alone. Respecting this need for personal space is vital for individual well-being.

Establish Boundaries: Set clear boundaries around personal time. This could mean designating certain evenings for individual activities or having "me time" on weekends. Communicating these boundaries ensures both partners feel valued.

Explore New Interests Together: Discover new hobbies or activities as a couple. This not only fosters togetherness but also allows you to grow and learn together, enhancing your connection.

Celebrate Individual Achievements: Acknowledge and celebrate each other's accomplishments, whether big or small. This reinforces the idea that you are supportive partners who value personal growth.

Check-In Regularly: Periodically assess how well you're balancing togetherness and individuality. Are both partners feeling fulfilled? Adjust as needed to ensure both needs are being met.

Practice Flexibility: Life can be unpredictable. Be open to shifting plans when needed, allowing for spontaneity in both shared and personal activities. Flexibility helps maintain a dynamic, responsive relationship.

Encourage Friendships: Support each other's friendships outside the relationship. Having strong social connections can enhance individual well-being, allowing both partners to return to the relationship rejuvenated.

Reflect and Adjust: Regularly reflect on your relationship dynamics. Are you feeling too close or too distant? Openly discussing these feelings can help recalibrate your balance.

Balancing togetherness and individuality is an ongoing journey that requires intention and effort. By embracing both shared experiences and personal time, you create a relationship that nurtures growth, fosters intimacy, and celebrates each partner's uniqueness. This delicate equilibrium not only strengthens your bond but also enriches your individual lives, leading to a fulfilling and harmonious partnership.

Embracing Individuality in Togetherness

As we conclude this chapter on the Law of Individuality, we invite you to reflect on the profound impact that embracing individuality can have on your relationship. When you honor each other's unique passions and aspirations, you cultivate a love that is both rich and resilient. This dynamic balance between togetherness and personal growth not only strengthens your bond but also inspires each partner to become the best version of themselves.

Imagine a relationship where both partners thrive, where shared moments are cherished and personal pursuits are celebrated. This is not just a dream; it's a possibility waiting to be realized. By committing to support each other's journeys, you create a partnership built on mutual respect, understanding, and love.

As you move forward, consider how you can apply the insights from this chapter in your own life. Reflect on your individual goals and interests, engage in open conversations with your partner, and

take actionable steps toward nurturing both your togetherness and your individuality. The journey of love is not merely about unity; it's about two unique souls dancing in harmony, each contributing their own rhythm to the relationship.

In the chapters that follow, we will explore more laws that deepen connections and foster resilience in love. Together, let's uncover the keys to building a relationship that not only stands the test of time but flourishes with passion, respect, and joy. Your adventure in love is just beginning—let's dive deeper into the transformative power of understanding and growth

10. The Grace of Forgiveness
- "Forgiveness: the key that unlocks the heart's freedom."

It is not merely a concept but a profound act that holds the power to heal wounds, mend hearts, and nurture the enduring bonds between partners. As we navigate the complexities of human connection, we inevitably encounter moments of hurt, misunderstanding, and disappointment. In these moments, the act of forgiveness becomes a transformative force, guiding us toward emotional well-being and the longevity of our relationships.

Forgiveness is often misunderstood as a simple act of absolution, yet it is far more nuanced. It is a conscious choice, a courageous step that allows us to release the burdens of resentment and anger. When we forgive, we free ourselves from the shackles of past grievances, creating space for growth, understanding, and deeper intimacy. It is a gentle reminder that love is not the absence of conflict, but the ability to rise above it with compassion and grace.

The healing power of forgiveness radiates through our emotional landscape, promoting resilience and well-being. When we harbor grudges, we cultivate a toxic environment within ourselves—one that breeds anxiety, stress, and even physical illness. By choosing to forgive, we reclaim our emotional freedom, allowing joy, peace, and love to flourish once again. In forgiving others, we also extend that grace to ourselves, acknowledging our own imperfections and vulnerabilities.

Moreover, the act of forgiveness serves as a cornerstone for lasting relationships. It fosters trust and creates an atmosphere of safety, where partners feel valued and understood. As we learn to navigate conflicts with empathy and patience, we strengthen the bonds that tie us together. Each act of forgiveness becomes a testament to our commitment to one another, reinforcing the belief that love can endure, evolve, and thrive, even in the face of adversity.

In this chapter, we will explore the transformative journey of forgiveness, understanding its importance not only for our emotional well-being but also for the vitality of our relationships. Through stories, reflections, and practical insights, we will uncover how embracing forgiveness can lead us to deeper connections and a more harmonious existence—both within ourselves and with those we hold dear.

The Law of Forgiveness: A Story of Devansh and Saanvi

In the heart of Jaipur, where the warm sun painted the ancient forts in shades of gold, lived a couple named Devansh and Saanvi. Their love story was woven with laughter, shared dreams, and moments that shimmered like the jewels for which their city was famous. But, like every relationship, theirs faced storms that tested the very foundation of their bond.

One evening, after a long day of work, Devansh returned home feeling overwhelmed. The pressures of his job had built up, and in a moment of frustration, he snapped at Saanvi during dinner. "Why can't you understand how hard I'm working?" he exclaimed, his voice echoing off the walls of their cozy home. Saanvi, taken aback, felt her heart sink. It was not the first time that stress had seeped into their conversations, but tonight it stung deeper.

Feeling hurt, Saanvi retreated to their balcony, gazing at the twinkling lights of the city. The vibrant colors of Jaipur, usually a source of inspiration, now felt distant. Devansh, realizing the weight of his words, followed her outside. The cool night air filled with an uncomfortable silence as he tried to find the right words to mend the rift.

"I'm sorry, Saanvi," he finally said, his voice softening. "I didn't mean to hurt you. I'm just feeling so overwhelmed." Saanvi turned to him, tears shimmering in her eyes. "I understand, Devansh, but I feel like I'm losing you to your stress. I just want to be there for you."

In that moment, something shifted. Instead of allowing resentment to build, they took a deep breath together. Devansh reached for Saanvi's hand, their fingers intertwining like the roots of an ancient tree. "Can we try to forgive each other?" he asked, vulnerability etched on his face.

Saanvi nodded, the weight of anger beginning to lift. "Forgiveness doesn't mean forgetting," she said gently. "It means we acknowledge the hurt but choose to move forward together." This was a pivotal moment for both of them. They recognized that forgiveness was not just a response to a mistake; it was a commitment to nurturing their relationship.

As the stars twinkled overhead, they shared their feelings, fears, and dreams, creating a space where vulnerability thrived. Devansh spoke of his anxiety about work, and Saanvi revealed her own insecurities about not being enough. Each word was a balm, soothing the wounds that had formed in the silence.

Over the following weeks, they made a conscious effort to practice forgiveness. Whenever tensions flared, they would pause and ask each other, "What do you need from me right now?" This simple question became a lifeline, allowing them to reconnect instead of drift apart.

One afternoon, as they strolled through the gardens of the City Palace, Saanvi spotted a vibrant flower. "Look, Devansh! It's like our love—it can bloom even in the harshest conditions." He smiled, taking in the beauty around them. "Yes, just like our relationship, it thrives with care and understanding."

Their bond deepened as they embraced forgiveness, transforming conflicts into opportunities for growth. With each act of understanding, they built a sturdy bridge over the chasms that once seemed insurmountable. The laughter that filled their home was now richer, and their moments together shimmered with newfound appreciation.

In time, Devansh and Saanvi learned that forgiveness was not just an occasional act; it became a daily practice, like watering a beloved plant. They discovered that by letting go of grudges and embracing each other's imperfections, they could cultivate a love that was resilient and beautiful.

As they celebrated their anniversary beneath the glowing sky, surrounded by friends and family, they shared their journey of forgiveness with those they loved. "It's not about never hurting each other," Saanvi spoke, her eyes bright with emotion. "It's about choosing to heal together, over and over again."

In that moment, Devansh knew that they had not just survived the storms; they had emerged stronger and more in love than ever before. Forgiveness had become their sanctuary, a reminder that in the dance of love, it is the grace of understanding that leads to the most beautiful steps.

As the city of Jaipur twinkled around them, Devansh and Saanvi embraced, knowing that their journey was just beginning, filled with endless possibilities and the promise of love that would always find a way to bloom.

Steps to Practice Forgiveness

Acknowledge Your Feelings: Allow yourself to fully feel the emotions associated with the hurt. Recognize anger, sadness, or disappointment without judgment.

Reflect on the Situation: Take time to understand what happened. Consider the context and motivations behind the actions that hurt you. This reflection can foster empathy.

Choose to Forgive: Make a conscious decision to forgive. This is a pivotal step that shifts your focus from resentment to healing.

Communicate Your Feelings: If possible, express your feelings to the person who hurt you. Open and honest communication can lead to mutual understanding.

Set Boundaries: Forgiveness doesn't mean you have to accept harmful behavior. Establish healthy boundaries to protect yourself while still letting go of resentment.

Let Go of Resentment: Understand that holding onto anger only harms you. Visualize releasing these feelings, whether through writing, talking, or a personal ritual.

Focus on the Present: Shift your attention from the past to the present moment. Engage in activities that bring you joy and fulfillment.

Practice Self-Compassion: Be kind to yourself throughout this process. Acknowledge that forgiveness is a journey, not a destination.

Seek Support: If necessary, talk to friends, family, or a therapist about your feelings. Sharing your journey can provide additional perspective and healing.

Revisit the Decision: Forgiveness is not always a one-time event. Check in with yourself periodically to reaffirm your decision to forgive as needed.

The Emotional Process of Forgiveness and Letting Go

Forgiveness is an emotional journey that unfolds in several stages:

Shock and Denial: Initially, when we experience hurt, we might feel stunned or unable to accept what happened. This is a natural protective response.

Anger and Resentment: As the reality sets in, feelings of anger and resentment often emerge. These emotions are valid and part of the healing process but can become toxic if not addressed.

Bargaining: We may find ourselves wishing for different circumstances or trying to negotiate with ourselves or the other person to undo the hurt. This phase often reflects our desire for control.

Reflection and Understanding: Gradually, we begin to reflect on the situation and consider the motivations behind the actions of others. This stage fosters empathy, which is crucial for moving toward forgiveness.

Acceptance: Acceptance is a pivotal emotional transition. It involves acknowledging the hurt while also recognizing that the past cannot be changed. This acceptance creates space for healing.

Decision to Forgive: At this stage, you consciously choose to forgive. This decision marks a shift from victimhood to empowerment, reclaiming your emotional well-being.

Letting Go: This is where true healing occurs. You actively release the negative emotions tied to the hurt, which allows you to move forward without the burden of resentment.

Rebuilding Trust: If the relationship is important to you, this phase involves working on rebuilding trust and connection, which may take time and effort.

Renewal and Growth: Forgiveness can lead to personal growth and transformation. You emerge with a deeper understanding of yourself and your relationships, often resulting in stronger, more resilient connections.

Practicing forgiveness is not just about freeing the other person from their mistakes; it's about liberating yourself from the emotional weight that can stifle your joy and hinder your relationships. Embracing this process can lead to a profound sense of peace, deeper connections, and a more fulfilling life.

Techniques for Letting Go of Resentment and Releasing Negative Feelings

Mindfulness and Meditation: Practicing mindfulness can help you become aware of your thoughts and feelings without judgment. Meditation allows you to create a calm space where you can process emotions and release negativity.

Journaling: Write about your feelings related to the resentment. Expressing your thoughts on paper can clarify your emotions and help you understand the root causes of your anger.

Visualization: Imagine letting go of the resentment. Visualize it as a heavy weight that you can release into the universe or as a balloon that you set free. This technique can create a sense of emotional liberation.

Affirmations: Use positive affirmations to reframe your mindset. Phrases like "I choose to release my anger and embrace peace" can reinforce your commitment to letting go.

Physical Activity: Engage in activities like yoga, running, or dancing. Physical movement helps release pent-up energy and can be a powerful outlet for negative emotions.

Talk It Out: Share your feelings with a trusted friend or therapist. Verbalizing your emotions can provide relief and offer new perspectives on the situation.

Practice Self-Compassion: Be kind to yourself. Acknowledge that it's normal to feel hurt and that healing takes time. Treat yourself with the same compassion you would offer a friend.

Create Boundaries: If someone consistently triggers negative feelings, set boundaries. Protecting yourself can help reduce resentment and promote emotional well-being.

Engage in Creative Expression: Channel your emotions into art, music, or writing. Creative outlets can help you process feelings and transform negativity into something positive.

Focus on Gratitude: Shift your perspective by cultivating gratitude. Make a list of things you appreciate in your life. Focusing on the positive can help diminish feelings of resentment.

Moving Forward

Embrace Change: Accept that moving on often requires change. Allow yourself to evolve, and be open to new experiences and relationships.

Set New Goals: Redirect your energy toward personal growth. Setting and working towards new goals can help you focus on the future rather than the past.

Practice Forgiveness: Remember that forgiveness is a continuous process. Revisit your commitment to forgive and remind yourself of the benefits it brings to your emotional health.

Build Positive Relationships: Surround yourself with supportive people who uplift you. Positive relationships can foster healing and reinforce a sense of belonging.

Cultivate Resilience: Work on developing emotional resilience. This involves learning from challenges, adapting to change, and maintaining a hopeful outlook.

Engage in New Experiences: Try new activities or hobbies that excite you. Engaging in fresh experiences can bring joy and help you move forward.

Reflect on Your Journey: Take time to acknowledge how far you've come. Reflecting on your progress can reinforce your commitment to moving forward and help you appreciate your growth.

Letting go of resentment is a courageous act that opens the door to healing and joy. By practicing these techniques, you can free yourself from negative emotions and create a brighter, more fulfilling future.

Conclusion: The Power of Forgiveness

As we conclude this chapter on the law of forgiveness, let us reflect on the profound transformation that comes from embracing this essential practice. Forgiveness is not simply an act of absolution; it is a powerful journey of healing that allows us to shed the heavy burdens of resentment and anger. It opens the door to emotional freedom and paves the way for deeper, more meaningful connections.

In our relationships, forgiveness fosters resilience, creating a sanctuary where love can flourish despite the inevitable storms we face. Each act of forgiveness serves as a reminder that we are all imperfect beings, capable of both hurt and healing. By choosing to forgive, we cultivate a space for empathy, understanding, and growth—both individually and together.

As you continue on your journey, remember that forgiveness is a daily practice, a choice that renews your commitment to love and connection. Embrace the beauty of letting go, and watch as your relationships transform into something more vibrant and enduring.

Take a moment to envision the life you want to lead—one filled with joy, acceptance, and authentic connection. The power to create that life lies within you. With each step you take towards forgiveness, you not only heal yourself but also inspire those around you to do the same.

So, dear reader, as you move forward, carry this law of forgiveness in your heart. Let it guide you through challenges and illuminate the path to deeper understanding and love. The journey may not always be easy, but the rewards are immeasurable. Embrace forgiveness as a guiding principle, and watch your world transform, one beautiful moment at a time.

11. The Language of Love
 - "Each love language is a whisper of the heart's desire."

Love is a language that doesn't need to be translated; it only needs to be felt. It's an ancient dialect, written in the rhythm of our hearts and spoken in ways far beyond mere words. While every relationship has its own unique lexicon, the language of love is universal—it speaks in the soft caress of a hand, the lingering gaze between two souls, and the quiet support in times of need. It's the secret vocabulary that binds lovers, creating an unspoken bond that transcends distance, time, and the limitations of language itself.

In this chapter, we'll journey through the delicate intricacies of how love communicates, not just through the words we say, but through the actions, the moments of silence, and the spaces between. True understanding in love comes when we begin to listen to its deeper expressions—when we tune in to the subtleties of our partner's needs, desires, and emotions.

From the spoken to the unspoken, from the gestures to the silences, the language of love is all around us, waiting to be understood. It is more than just a tool for connection; it is the essence of the relationship itself. When we learn to speak this language fluently, we unlock a world of intimacy and understanding that transforms our connections and elevates our love to a deeper, more profound level.

So, as we delve into the poetry of love's language, prepare to open your heart and mind to its many forms. This chapter will show you how to not just hear, but truly listen to the most beautiful conversation two people can ever have—one of love.

Dev and Isha: A Love Story

In the heart of Varanasi, where the holy Ganga flows gracefully and life unfolds in vibrant colors, Dev and Isha found each other amidst the chaos of daily life. They were young, ambitious, and deeply in love, yet their relationship faced challenges, often stemming from their different ways of expressing love.

Dev was a man of few words. He believed actions spoke louder than any compliment. He was the type who would quietly take care of chores, help his friends with their projects, and surprise Isha with her favorite snacks after a long day at work. However, Isha craved verbal affirmation. She

wanted to hear him express his love, to be reminded of how much she meant to him. When Dev would simply smile or nod, Isha often felt that her feelings went unacknowledged.

One evening, as they sat by the banks of the Ganges, the sun setting in a blaze of orange and pink, Isha decided it was time to talk. "Dev," she began, her voice soft yet firm, "I love how you always help me when I'm stressed, but sometimes I wish you would just tell me you love me."

Dev looked at her, surprised. "I thought you knew how I felt. I show you love in my own way."

"I do know, but hearing it makes me feel cherished. It's just how I feel loved," Isha explained.

Dev listened intently. This moment was a revelation for him; he realized they spoke different love languages. He wanted to learn to express his love in a way that resonated with Isha.

From that day, Dev made a conscious effort to incorporate words of affirmation into their relationship. He began leaving sweet notes for Isha to find, expressing his feelings in simple yet heartfelt phrases. "You make my world brighter," one note read, and another simply stated, "I love you, Isha." Each time she found one, her heart swelled with happiness.

Meanwhile, Isha recognized Dev's love language, Acts of Service. She began to appreciate the little things he did, like cleaning up after dinner or preparing her favorite tea. Instead of merely focusing on what she wanted, she made an effort to acknowledge his actions. "Thank you for always being there for me," she would say, her eyes sparkling with gratitude.

As they continued to navigate their relationship, Isha introduced Quality Time into their routine. They started setting aside Sunday afternoons for long walks along the Ganga, talking about their dreams and aspirations. These moments became sacred, allowing them to connect on a deeper level. Dev loved the way Isha's laughter echoed against the water, and Isha cherished the peaceful silence they sometimes shared, simply enjoying each other's presence.

With time, Dev also embraced the importance of Receiving Gifts. He surprised Isha on her birthday with a handmade scrapbook filled with memories they had created together— ticket stubs, photos, and little notes. "This is my way of showing you how much you mean to me," he said, watching her eyes light up.

Physical Touch was another aspect of their relationship that blossomed. Isha found comfort in Dev's hugs, and she initiated cuddles during their movie nights. Dev, too, learned to express his love through these small gestures, often intertwining his fingers with hers as they walked.

Together, they created a beautiful love, woven with their unique languages. Dev learned that words could bring a warmth that actions sometimes couldn't, while Isha discovered the depth of love found in simple acts of kindness. They realized that love wasn't about changing one another but rather understanding and embracing each other's differences.

In the heart of Varanasi, under the shimmering lights of the ghats, Dev and Isha built a relationship that thrived on understanding and appreciation. By learning to speak each other's love languages, they transformed their bond into something beautiful and enduring—a testament to the power of love, patience, and open communication.

As the Ganga continued to flow, so did their love, ever evolving and deepening with each passing day.

Integrating Love Languages into Daily Life

Understanding and incorporating love languages into your daily routine can significantly enhance your connection with your partner. Here are practical tips to help you integrate love languages seamlessly into your lives:

Daily Affirmations (Words of Affirmation

Tip: Start each day by complimenting your partner or expressing appreciation. A simple "I love how you always support me" or "You make me so happy" can set a positive tone.

Practice: Leave sticky notes with loving messages in places your partner will find them, like on the bathroom mirror or in their lunch.

Acts of Service as Love

Tip: Identify specific tasks your partner finds burdensome and take the initiative to do them. This could be anything from doing the dishes to picking up groceries.

Practice: Create a shared chores list and take turns completing each other's least favorite tasks. This not only lightens the load but shows your partner you care.

Thoughtful Gifts

Tip: Surprise your partner with small, thoughtful gifts that show you're thinking of them. It doesn't have to be expensive—consider their favorite snack or a book you know they'll love.

Practice: Set a monthly goal to give each other a surprise gift. It can be something simple, like a handwritten letter or a favorite treat.

Quality Time Rituals

Tip: Schedule regular "date nights" or dedicated time together without distractions. This could be as simple as cooking dinner together or taking a walk.

Practice: Create a weekly tradition, like Sunday brunch or an evening stroll. Make it a tech-free time to deepen your conversation and connection.

Physical Touch

Tip: Make physical affection a priority. This can include holding hands, hugs, cuddling on the couch, or gentle touches throughout the day.

Practice: Set aside a few minutes each day for intentional physical connection. Whether it's a long hug or cuddling during a movie, make it a regular habit.

Mindful Communication

Tip: During conversations, focus on actively listening and engaging with your partner's feelings. Acknowledge their expressions of love and share yours in return.

Practice: During your quality time, set aside a few minutes to share what makes you feel loved and how you can reciprocate. This openness fosters intimacy.

Incorporate Love Languages into Special Occasions

Tip: On birthdays, anniversaries, or other special occasions, tailor your celebrations to include your partner's love languages. For example, write a heartfelt letter (Words of Affirmation) and plan a surprise outing (Quality Time).

Practice: Create a tradition where you both share your love languages during special occasions, ensuring that each celebration resonates deeply with both partners.

Express Gratitude

Tip: Regularly express gratitude for the ways your partner shows love. This reinforces positive behavior and encourages them to continue expressing their love language.

Practice: Keep a gratitude journal where you note the little things your partner does for you. Share entries with each other during your quality time.

Incorporating love languages into daily life is about creating habits that strengthen your connection and understanding of one another. By being intentional and thoughtful in your actions, you not only nurture your relationship but also create a deeper, more fulfilling bond. As you integrate these practices, you'll likely find that your love for each other deepens, leading to a more harmonious and loving partnership.

Conclusion

it's essential to recognize the profound impact understanding these languages can have on our relationships. Just like Dev and Isha, each couple navigates the ebb and flow of connection, sometimes lost in translation yet always yearning to be understood. By embracing the unique ways we express love—whether through words, actions, gifts, time, or touch—we create an environment where love can flourish.

Love is not a one-size-fits-all experience; it is a delicate dance that thrives on communication, empathy, and the willingness to learn. This book has journeyed through the many facets of love, equipping you with the insights to nurture and deepen your connections. It serves as a reminder that love is an art—one that requires patience, practice, and an open heart.

As you embark on your own journey of love, may you discover the beauty in each gesture, the power in each word, and the warmth in each embrace. Let this chapter inspire you to explore the love languages within your relationship, fostering a connection that is not only meaningful but also transformative.

In the end, love is the greatest language of all, transcending barriers and uniting hearts. Embrace it, celebrate it, and watch as it transforms your relationships into something truly magnificent. Thank you for being part of this exploration—may your journey of love be rich, rewarding, and endlessly beautiful.

115

12. The Depth of Empathy
- "To understand is to love; to love is to understand."

Empathy is the cornerstone of meaningful relationships, serving as a bridge that connects us to others on a profound emotional level. At its core, empathy is the ability to understand and share the feelings of another person. It goes beyond mere sympathy; while sympathy involves feeling compassion for someone else's situation, empathy requires us to step into their shoes, to perceive the world through their eyes, and to feel their emotions as if they were our own.

Understanding empathy involves recognizing its two primary components: cognitive empathy and emotional empathy. Cognitive empathy allows us to comprehend what someone else is feeling, to grasp their perspective, and to acknowledge their experiences without judgment. Emotional empathy, on the other hand, enables us to resonate with those feelings, fostering a deeper emotional connection. Together, these facets create a holistic understanding of another's emotional landscape.

The significance of empathy in fostering connection cannot be overstated. When we practice empathy, we cultivate an atmosphere of trust and safety. This encourages open communication, allowing partners to share their vulnerabilities without fear of rejection. Empathy helps to dissolve barriers and misunderstandings, transforming conflicts into opportunities for growth and intimacy. In relationships, it acts as a balm for wounds, facilitating healing and reconciliation.

As we explore the law of empathy in this chapter, we will uncover practical ways to nurture this essential skill, emphasizing that empathy is not merely an innate trait but a practice we can all develop. By embracing empathy, we create a rich tapestry of connection that binds us together, allowing love to flourish in its truest form.

The Power of Empathy: The Story of Vihaan and Sneha

In the bustling streets of Agra, beneath the shadow of the majestic Taj Mahal, lived Vihaan and Sneha—a couple whose love story was as intricate and beautiful as the architecture that surrounded them. Both in their early twenties, they were a vibrant reflection of their city, blending tradition with modernity, yet they faced challenges that threatened to pull them apart.

Vihaan was a budding architect, passionate about his work but often consumed by the pressures of deadlines. Sneha, an aspiring artist, sought to express herself through her paintings but struggled with feelings of inadequacy. While they loved each other deeply, the stress of their individual pursuits began to create a chasm between them. Misunderstandings crept in, and small arguments became frequent, leaving both feeling isolated in their own worlds.

One rainy evening, after a particularly heated argument about a missed dinner date, Vihaan sat alone in his room, staring blankly at his sketches. The rain pattered against the window, mirroring the turmoil in his heart. He felt a wave of frustration, but deep down, he also felt guilt for not being more understanding of Sneha's struggles.

Sneha, too, was feeling the weight of the argument. She wandered through the narrow lanes of Agra, her thoughts spiraling into self-doubt. She reached the banks of the Yamuna River, where they often spent evenings together. Sitting there, she realized that her passion for art was often overshadowed by her insecurities, and she longed for Vihaan's support, not just as a partner but as a friend.

The next day, Vihaan decided to take a step toward bridging the gap between them. He arranged a small surprise picnic by the river, hoping to reconnect. When Sneha arrived, her initial surprise quickly turned into a warm smile as she saw the spread he had laid out—her favorite snacks, a cozy blanket, and even a few art supplies.

As they settled down, the air was filled with the fragrance of freshly baked samosas and the sound of laughter. Vihaan turned to Sneha, his eyes earnest. "I've been thinking a lot about us," he began, his voice softer than usual. "I realize I haven't been there for you like I should. I get so caught up in my work that I forget to ask how you're feeling. I'm really sorry."

Sneha looked into his eyes, surprised but touched by his sincerity. "I've been struggling too," she admitted, her voice quivering slightly. "I want to share my art with you, but I often feel like it's not good enough. I wish you could see how much it means to me."

In that moment, something shifted between them. Vihaan took Sneha's hand, squeezing it gently. "You are incredible, Sneha. I want to be there for you—to understand your passion, your struggles. Let's share our worlds more."

They spent the afternoon talking openly, sharing their fears and dreams. Vihaan listened intently as Sneha spoke about her art, her voice gradually gaining strength and confidence. Likewise, Sneha asked Vihaan about his projects, and for the first time in weeks, he felt seen and supported.

From that day forward, empathy became the foundation of their relationship. They learned to communicate openly, checking in with each other about their feelings and struggles. Vihaan would accompany Sneha to her art exhibitions, offering encouragement and support. Sneha, in turn, would often bring him coffee during late-night work sessions, reminding him to take breaks and care for himself.

As they continued to practice empathy, their bond deepened. They discovered that understanding each other's perspectives not only helped them navigate challenges but also enriched their love. They celebrated each other's victories, no matter how small, and faced setbacks together, stronger as a team.

Months later, as they stood together on the terrace of their home, overlooking the illuminated Taj Mahal, Vihaan turned to Sneha. "You know, I used to think that love was just about passion and romance," he said, his voice filled with warmth. "But now I know it's about understanding, about truly being there for one another."

Sneha smiled, her heart full. "And that's what makes us stronger. Our love isn't just a feeling; it's an ongoing choice to connect deeply, to be empathetic."

In that moment, beneath the stars and the glow of their beloved city, Vihaan and Sneha realized that their relationship had transformed into a beautiful, resilient bond—one that was rooted in empathy, understanding, and unconditional support. And as they embraced, they knew they had created something timeless, just like the monument that symbolized their love.

Vihaan and Sneha's story illustrates the profound impact of empathy in a relationship. By learning to listen, understand, and support each other, they turned their challenges into opportunities for

growth, strengthening their bond in ways they never imagined possible. In love, empathy is not just an ideal; it's a practice—a vital law that nurtures connection and fosters lasting harmony.

The Role of Empathy in Conflict Resolution

Empathy plays a crucial role in resolving conflicts, serving as a powerful tool to de-escalate tensions and promote mutual understanding. When individuals approach conflicts with empathy, they create a space where open communication and collaboration can flourish. Here's how empathy can facilitate conflict resolution:

Understanding Different Perspectives

De-escalation: Empathy allows individuals to see the conflict from multiple angles. By actively trying to understand the other person's feelings and motivations, we can diffuse misunderstandings that often escalate tensions.

Promoting Understanding: When each party feels heard and understood, it can reduce feelings of frustration or anger, paving the way for constructive dialogue.

Emotional Validation

De-escalation: Acknowledging the emotions of others is a key aspect of empathy. When people feel that their feelings are recognized and validated, they are less likely to react defensively.

Promoting Understanding: By expressing empathy, you can reassure the other person that their feelings are legitimate. This can foster an environment where both parties feel safe to express their concerns and emotions openly.

Encouraging Open Communication

De-escalation: Empathy fosters a non-judgmental space where individuals are more likely to share their thoughts and feelings honestly. This can prevent the buildup of resentment that often leads to more significant conflicts.

Promoting Understanding: By encouraging dialogue and open communication, empathy allows for the exploration of underlying issues rather than focusing solely on surface-level disagreements.

Facilitating Problem-Solving

De-escalation: When conflicts arise, empathy shifts the focus from blame to collaboration. By working together to understand each other's needs and desires, parties can collaboratively identify solutions.

Promoting Understanding: Empathetic communication helps both sides identify common goals, leading to solutions that are acceptable to everyone involved.

Building Trust and Rapport

De-escalation: Empathy can help to establish a foundation of trust, making it easier for individuals to engage in constructive conflict resolution rather than resorting to hostility.

Promoting Understanding: Trust fosters an atmosphere where individuals feel valued and respected. When people trust one another, they are more willing to engage in honest discussions and seek resolutions.

Reducing Defensiveness

De-escalation: When individuals approach conflicts with empathy, it often reduces the likelihood of defensive reactions. Instead of feeling attacked, they feel understood, which helps to lower their guard.

Promoting Understanding: This reduction in defensiveness allows for a more open exchange of ideas and feelings, facilitating a greater willingness to compromise and collaborate.

Encouraging Reflection

De-escalation: Empathy encourages individuals to reflect on their own actions and how those might have contributed to the conflict. This self-awareness can lead to personal growth and change.

Promoting Understanding: Reflecting on one's own role in a conflict allows for a deeper understanding of how our actions affect others, fostering accountability and growth.

Empathy is a vital component of effective conflict resolution. By promoting understanding, reducing defensiveness, and encouraging open communication, empathy can transform conflicts from adversarial confrontations into opportunities for collaboration and connection. When individuals practice empathy, they create a more harmonious environment where differences can be resolved constructively, ultimately leading to stronger and more resilient relationships.

The Transformative Power of Empathy

As we conclude our exploration of the Law of Empathy, it becomes clear that this profound skill is not merely an enhancement of our relationships; it is the very foundation upon which love flourishes. Through empathy, we learn to embrace each other's perspectives, validate each other's feelings, and foster a deep, abiding connection that transcends misunderstandings and conflict.

empathy acts as a vibrant thread, weaving together our individual experiences and emotions into a rich, harmonious whole. It invites us to step outside ourselves, to listen with our hearts, and to respond with compassion. This practice transforms not just our relationships but also ourselves, guiding us toward greater awareness and deeper connections.

As you continue your journey through this book, may you carry the lessons of empathy close to your heart. Remember that love is a continuous process—a choice we make every day. By cultivating empathy, we nurture not only our partnerships but also the very essence of what it means to love and be loved.

In the end, investing in empathy is investing in the beauty of your relationships. It opens doors to understanding, healing, and growth. As you practice these principles, you'll find that love becomes not just an emotion but a living, breathing connection that enriches your life in countless ways. Embrace this journey, for in the realm of love, there is always more to discover, and the rewards are boundless. Your heart—and the hearts of those you cherish—will thank you for it

13. The Light of Honesty

- "Truth is the beacon that guides us through the storms."

Honesty is the foundation upon which the most profound relationships are built. It is not merely the absence of deceit, but an active commitment to transparency and truthfulness. When partners embrace honesty, they create a safe space where vulnerability can flourish, enabling deeper connections and a more authentic love.

The impact of honesty in relationships is profound. When each person feels free to express their true thoughts and feelings without fear of judgment or reprisal, trust blossoms. This trust becomes the bedrock of the relationship, fostering a sense of security that allows both individuals to open up fully. In this atmosphere, partners are more likely to share their hopes, fears, and dreams, leading to a greater understanding of one another.

Moreover, honesty paves the way for effective communication. It encourages the practice of expressing needs and boundaries clearly, reducing misunderstandings and conflicts. When both partners are committed to honesty, they are more equipped to address issues head-on, transforming potential obstacles into opportunities for growth.

Honesty also cultivates resilience. In times of hardship, knowing that your partner is truthful creates a sense of unity. Challenges are faced together, with a shared understanding that each person is committed to the relationship's well-being. This collaboration, rooted in honesty, strengthens the bond between partners, reinforcing their connection through shared experiences.

Ultimately, the law of honesty reminds us that love is not just about the grand gestures, but also about the everyday truths we share with one another. It encourages us to be our authentic selves and to honor that authenticity in our partners. In doing so, we build a relationship that is not only strong and resilient but also deeply fulfilling.

As you navigate the complexities of love, remember that honesty is a powerful ally. It deepens trust, enhances communication, and fortifies the bond between partners. In the realm of love, honesty is not just a law; it is a guiding principle that lights the path toward a lasting and meaningful connection.

The Heart of Honesty: Arman and Zara

In the vibrant city of Lucknow, where the air was filled with the scent of biryani and the echoes of laughter, lived a couple named Arman and Zara. Their love story blossomed amidst the bustling streets, adorned with the rich heritage of their culture. From their first meeting at a local café, it was clear that they shared a unique connection, a bond strengthened by mutual respect and understanding.

As their relationship deepened, Arman and Zara embraced the importance of honesty. They believed that being truthful with each other was not just about avoiding deception but about fostering an environment where both felt safe to express their innermost thoughts and feelings.

One evening, while watching the sunset over the Gomti River, Zara noticed a change in Arman's demeanor. He seemed distant, lost in thought. Concerned, she gently prompted him to share what was on his mind. After a moment of hesitation, Arman opened up about a recent job offer he received that would require him to move to another city.

"I'm excited about the opportunity," he confessed, "but I'm torn. I don't want to leave you behind."

Zara felt a rush of emotions, but instead of reacting impulsively, she took a deep breath. "Thank you for telling me, Arman. I appreciate your honesty. It's a big decision, and I want you to follow your dreams, but I also need to understand how it affects us."

This open dialogue marked a turning point in their relationship. Instead of hiding their fears or pretending that everything was fine, they faced the uncertainty together. They spent hours discussing their dreams, hopes, and the possibility of a long-distance relationship. With each conversation, they realized that their honesty brought them closer, allowing them to navigate challenges with empathy and support.

As time passed, the couple faced more trials—a misunderstanding about finances, differing opinions on social outings, and the inevitable ups and downs of life. Yet, each time they encountered a hurdle, they chose to communicate openly. Zara learned to voice her feelings without fear, while Arman practiced listening without judgment.

One rainy afternoon, they found themselves caught in a heated argument. Emotions ran high, and Zara felt overwhelmed. Instead of letting the anger fester, she took a step back and asked, "Can we pause for a moment? I need to be honest with you about how I'm feeling."

Arman nodded, realizing that this was a crucial moment. "I'm sorry for raising my voice. I want to understand your perspective."

This simple act of pausing to communicate honestly transformed their conflict into an opportunity for growth. They not only resolved their disagreement but also learned more about each other's backgrounds and values, strengthening their connection.

As the months turned into years, Arman and Zara's love matured. They celebrated each milestone, big and small, and supported one another's aspirations. Through it all, their commitment to honesty created an unshakeable foundation. They realized that honesty was not just about telling the truth but about fostering trust and vulnerability.

On the day of their engagement, as they stood surrounded by family and friends in a beautiful Lucknow courtyard, Arman held Zara's hands and smiled. "I promise to always be honest with you, to share my dreams and fears, and to cherish the bond we've built."

Zara's eyes sparkled with tears of joy. "And I promise to do the same. Our honesty has brought us this far, and I believe it will guide us through whatever comes next."

In that moment, they knew their relationship was stronger than ever—a beautiful testament to the power of honesty. Together, they embarked on their journey into the future, hand in hand, ready to face the world, knowing that their love was rooted in truth and understanding.

Balancing Honesty with Kindness: The Art of Compassionate Feedback

In any relationship, honesty is vital for growth and trust, but delivering truthful feedback can sometimes be challenging. Striking the right balance between honesty and kindness is essential for ensuring that feedback is both constructive and compassionate. Here's why this balance matters and how to achieve it.

The Importance of Compassionate Feedback

Fostering Trust: When feedback is delivered with kindness, it builds trust. Recipients are more likely to feel safe and valued, knowing that their feelings are considered. This trust encourages open communication and a willingness to engage in difficult conversations.

Encouraging Growth: Honest feedback is crucial for personal and relational growth. However, when it's delivered harshly, it can lead to defensiveness or resentment. Compassionate feedback helps the recipient understand the intent behind the message, making them more receptive to change.

Preserving Relationships: In any relationship, the way feedback is communicated can significantly impact the connection between individuals. Kindness ensures that the message is not just heard but also appreciated, preserving the integrity of the relationship even when difficult truths are discussed.

Promoting Emotional Well-Being: Kindness can mitigate the emotional impact of critical feedback. When people receive feedback in a gentle manner, they are more likely to feel supported rather than attacked. This can enhance their overall well-being and willingness to engage in future discussions.

How to Deliver Honest Feedback with Compassion

Choose the Right Moment: Timing can make a significant difference. Find a calm, private setting to share feedback, ensuring that both parties can engage without distractions or heightened emotions.

Use "I" Statements: Frame feedback from your perspective. For example, instead of saying, "You never listen to me," try, "I feel unheard when we talk." This approach reduces defensiveness and emphasizes personal feelings rather than accusations.

Focus on Behavior, Not Character: Address specific behaviors rather than making blanket statements about a person's character. For instance, instead of saying, "You're disorganized," you could say, "I've noticed some details were missed in the last project. How can we work on that together?"

Balance Positives with Negatives: Begin with positive observations before introducing areas for improvement. This technique, often referred to as the "sandwich method," helps soften the blow of critical feedback by framing it within a context of appreciation.

Encourage Dialogue: Invite the recipient to share their perspective. This not only shows respect for their feelings but also opens the floor for a more collaborative discussion. Phrasing like, "What are your thoughts on this?" fosters a two-way conversation.

Express Empathy: Acknowledge the recipient's feelings and experiences. Simple phrases like, "I understand this may be difficult to hear," can validate their emotions and show that you care about their well-being.

Offer Support: Conclude with a willingness to help. Whether it's providing resources, brainstorming solutions, or simply being there to listen, offering support reinforces your commitment to their growth and success.

Balancing honesty with kindness is an essential skill in any relationship. By delivering truthful feedback with compassion, we foster trust, encourage growth, and strengthen our connections. In the end, the goal of feedback should always be to uplift and empower rather than to criticize or diminish. When honesty is coupled with kindness, it transforms difficult conversations into opportunities for understanding and connection, paving the way for healthier, more resilient relationships.

Embracing the Law of Honesty

As we draw this chapter to a close, let us reflect on the profound beauty that honesty brings to our relationships. In a world often filled with noise and distractions, the commitment to truth stands as a beacon of light, guiding us toward deeper connections and greater understanding. Honesty is not just a principle; it is an invitation to be truly seen and heard, a pathway to intimacy that nourishes our hearts.

When we choose honesty, we create a sanctuary where vulnerability can thrive. We allow ourselves to show our authentic selves, embracing both our strengths and imperfections. This openness fosters trust—a delicate thread that weaves our hearts closer together. Trust, once established, becomes the foundation upon which we build our dreams, navigate challenges, and celebrate our victories.

Remember, honesty is a journey, not a destination. It requires courage to speak our truths and the kindness to hear them. It challenges us to confront discomfort and to approach each other with empathy. As you and your partner embark on this path, cherish the moments of honest communication, knowing that each conversation is a step toward a richer, more fulfilling relationship.

So, let us commit to nurturing this law of honesty in our lives. Let us speak our truths with compassion, listen with open hearts, and create spaces where love can flourish. In doing so, we not only strengthen our bonds but also inspire those around us to embrace their own journeys of honesty.

May your hearts be filled with courage and your conversations be infused with love. Together, let us build relationships that celebrate authenticity, knowing that in honesty lies the power to transform not only ourselves but also the world around us.

14. The Journey of Growth

- "In love, we blossom; in unity, we flourish."

In any healthy partnership, growth is essential. Just as individuals evolve, so too must their relationships. This chapter explores the importance of growth in love, emphasizing how personal and relational development enriches partnerships.

The Importance of Growth

Growth in relationships is a dynamic process that fosters deeper connections and enhances mutual understanding. It is a continuous journey where both partners evolve, learning from experiences and adapting to changes. This growth can manifest in various ways—emotionally, intellectually, spiritually, and socially.

Personal Growth: When individuals commit to personal growth, they become more self-aware and emotionally intelligent. This self-improvement positively impacts the relationship, as partners bring their best selves to the partnership. Personal growth fosters resilience, allowing partners to navigate challenges more effectively.

Relational Growth: Relationships, like living organisms, require nurturing to thrive. Relational growth involves cultivating emotional intimacy, improving communication skills, and building trust. When both partners actively work on the relationship, it becomes a safe space for vulnerability and support.

Enriching the Partnership

Enhanced Communication: Growth encourages open dialogue. As individuals develop, they learn to articulate their needs, desires, and concerns more effectively. This clarity fosters understanding and reduces conflicts.

Deeper Connection: As partners grow, they often discover new dimensions of themselves and each other. This exploration deepens emotional bonds, allowing for shared experiences that enhance intimacy and trust.

Shared Goals and Values: Personal growth can lead to the reassessment of life goals and values. When partners align their aspirations, they create a shared vision for the future, strengthening their commitment and collaboration.

Adaptability to Change: Life is full of transitions—career changes, family dynamics, and personal challenges. Growth equips partners with the flexibility to adapt to these changes together, reinforcing their partnership.

Increased Resilience: Growth fosters a mindset that views challenges as opportunities for learning. This resilience can buffer against the inevitable stresses that relationships face, helping couples to emerge stronger.

In summary, the law of growth underscores that a thriving relationship is one where both partners are committed to their personal and relational development. By investing in growth, couples not only enrich their own lives but also enhance the partnership, creating a lasting bond built on understanding, respect, and shared aspirations. Growth is not merely a goal but a lifelong journey that transforms love into a profound and fulfilling experience.

Vignesh and Sneha: A Journey of Growth

In the vibrant city of Coimbatore, Vignesh and Sneha shared a love that was as warm and inviting as the southern sun. They met during college, their connection blossoming over shared classes and late-night study sessions. Initially, their relationship was a delightful whirlwind of laughter and youthful romance, filled with dreams of the future.

However, as time passed, they began to realize that love was not just about shared moments but also about growth—both personal and relational.

The Early Days

In their early relationship, Vignesh was a spirited young man with ambitions in engineering, while Sneha, an aspiring artist, poured her heart into her canvases. They cherished their differences, often discussing their dreams late into the night. Yet, as they approached graduation, the pressures of the future began to weigh heavily on them.

Vignesh secured a job in a prestigious firm, while Sneha struggled to find her footing in the art world. The transition was challenging; Vignesh was consumed by his new responsibilities, and Sneha felt increasingly isolated as her passion became overshadowed by self-doubt. They began to drift apart, their once vibrant conversations turning into awkward silences.

The Turning Point

Recognizing the growing distance, Sneha decided to confront the issue. One evening, she invited Vignesh to their favorite café, where they first met. With a trembling heart, she expressed her feelings. "I feel like we're growing apart, Vignesh. I miss the way we used to share our dreams. I need you to be present in this journey with me."

Vignesh listened intently, his heart heavy with realization. He acknowledged that he had been so focused on his career that he neglected the emotional connection they had built. This moment became a catalyst for change; both understood that they needed to grow—not just individually, but together.

Embracing Growth

Determined to strengthen their bond, Vignesh and Sneha committed to fostering both personal and relational growth. They began setting aside time for each other every week, engaging in activities that inspired them. Vignesh started attending art exhibitions with Sneha, and she, in turn, supported him during his work projects, even helping him brainstorm ideas.

They also encouraged each other to pursue personal goals. Sneha enrolled in art workshops, gaining confidence and skill, while Vignesh sought mentorship at work, learning to navigate the corporate landscape with greater ease. Each achievement brought them closer, as they celebrated successes and learned from setbacks together.

Building a Strong Bond

As they continued to grow, Vignesh and Sneha discovered deeper layers of love and understanding. They learned to communicate openly, sharing their fears and aspirations without judgment. Their relationship flourished as they built a foundation of trust and respect.

One day, while walking through the lush botanical gardens of Coimbatore, Sneha turned to Vignesh, her eyes sparkling with excitement. "I just got accepted into a prestigious art show! I can't believe it!" she exclaimed. Vignesh beamed with pride, wrapping her in a warm embrace. "You deserve it, Sneha. Your passion inspires me every day."

In that moment, they both realized how their individual growth had enriched their partnership. Each success was no longer a solitary victory but a shared joy that reinforced their bond.

A Future Together

Years later, Vignesh and Sneha stood hand in hand at their wedding, surrounded by friends and family. As they exchanged vows, they reflected on their journey—a testament to the importance of growth in love. They promised to continue evolving together, to support each other's dreams, and to nurture their love through all of life's changes.

Their story became a beautiful narrative of how personal and relational growth can transform a relationship into something profound and lasting. Vignesh and Sneha learned that love is not just about the moments shared but about the growth experienced together, building a strong, enduring bond that could weather any storm. And in Coimbatore, their love story became a beacon of hope for others, illustrating that true love thrives on the journey of growth.

Adapting to Life Changes: Navigating Transitions Together

Life is a series of changes, and navigating them as a couple can be both challenging and enriching. Adapting to these changes while maintaining a strong connection is crucial for the health of your relationship. Here are some effective strategies couples can use to face life's transitions together:

1. Embrace Open Communication

Share Feelings and Concerns: When changes arise—be it a job loss, relocation, or family changes—discuss your feelings openly. Sharing anxieties and expectations can help both partners feel understood and supported.

Practice Active Listening: Ensure that both partners feel heard. Encourage each other to express thoughts without interruption, validating each other's feelings in the process.

2. Maintain a Supportive Environment

Be Each Other's Anchor: Offer emotional support during challenging times. Whether it's a listening ear or a comforting gesture, being present for each other fosters a sense of security.

Encourage Independence: While supporting each other is essential, also encourage personal growth and independence. Allow each other to pursue individual interests or seek external support when needed.

3. Create a Shared Action Plan

Set Goals Together: When facing a significant change, create a plan that outlines how you will navigate the transition. Define short-term and long-term goals, and discuss how you can achieve them together.

Divide Responsibilities: Assign roles based on each partner's strengths. This division of tasks can help manage stress and foster teamwork, making the transition feel more manageable.

4. Prioritize Quality Time

Stay Connected: In the midst of change, prioritize time together. This could be regular date nights, walks, or even simple conversations at the end of the day. These moments reinforce your bond.

Engage in Shared Activities: Find new activities that you can explore together, whether it's a new hobby, cooking together, or taking a class. Shared experiences can strengthen your connection and bring joy amidst uncertainty.

5. Practice Patience and Flexibility

Be Patient with Each Other: Understand that adapting to change takes time. Allow space for each other to process emotions and adjust at their own pace.

Stay Flexible: Life changes can be unpredictable. Embrace flexibility in your plans and expectations, which can reduce frustration and help you adapt more easily.

6. Reassess and Realign

Check In Regularly: Make it a habit to check in with each other about how you're feeling regarding the change. This ongoing dialogue can help you both stay aligned and address any issues before they escalate.

Adapt Your Goals: As circumstances evolve, be open to reassessing your goals and aspirations. Ensure that they reflect your current situation and align with your shared vision.

7. Celebrate Small Wins

Acknowledge Progress: Celebrate achievements, no matter how small, as you navigate changes. Recognizing progress reinforces your commitment to each other and boosts morale.

Create Rituals: Establish small rituals or traditions that mark your journey through change. This could be a special dinner, a toast, or simply reflecting on your experiences together. These moments create positive associations and strengthen your bond.

Adapting to life changes is a fundamental aspect of any relationship. By embracing open communication, supporting one another, and prioritizing your connection, couples can navigate transitions more smoothly. Remember, it's not just about the challenges you face, but how you face them together that can ultimately deepen your bond and enrich your partnership. Through patience, teamwork, and celebration, you can emerge from changes stronger and more connected than ever.

Conclusion: Embracing the Journey of Love

As we conclude this exploration of love, relationships, and the principles that guide them, it's important to reflect on the journey you've undertaken throughout this book. Each chapter has offered insights into the complexities of love, highlighting the importance of communication, growth, shared goals, and adaptability. These themes are not merely concepts to be understood; they are the lifeblood of a thriving partnership.

Love is a beautiful and dynamic force, one that requires dedication, vulnerability, and an unwavering commitment to each other. By embracing the lessons shared here, you are equipped to nurture your relationship, creating a foundation that not only withstands the tests of time but flourishes in the face of change.

Remember, every relationship is unique, shaped by the individual experiences and aspirations of those within it. As you move forward, take the time to envision your future together, set mutual goals, and celebrate the journey—both the challenges and triumphs. Cherish the small moments of connection, for they weave the rich tapestry of your shared life.

Thank you for joining me on this exploration of love and relationships. May the insights gained from this book empower you to create a partnership that is resilient, fulfilling, and deeply rewarding. As you embark on the next chapter of your love story, know that the journey of understanding, growing, and loving is one of the most profound adventures you can undertake together. Here's to love, in all its forms, and to the beautiful journey that lies ahead.

15. The Warmth of Intimacy
- "Intimacy is the sacred space where souls connect."

Intimacy is the heartbeat of any romantic relationship, embodying both emotional and physical dimensions that intertwine to create a deep connection between partners. As we delve into the intricate landscape of intimacy, it's essential to recognize how these two forms interact and contribute to a relationship's strength and resilience.

Emotional Intimacy refers to the closeness that emerges from sharing thoughts, feelings, and vulnerabilities with one another. It is built on trust, empathy, and understanding, allowing partners to communicate openly without fear of judgment. This type of intimacy fosters a safe space where both individuals can express their true selves, facilitating a profound bond that often transcends superficial interactions. The significance of emotional intimacy lies in its ability to cultivate a sense of belonging and security, providing a foundation that enhances mutual respect and affection.

Physical Intimacy, on the other hand, encompasses the tangible expressions of love and affection, ranging from tender touches to passionate encounters. This type of intimacy can serve as a powerful language of connection, often reinforcing emotional bonds through shared physical experiences. Physical intimacy is not solely about sexual interactions; it includes gestures of affection, such as holding hands, cuddling, or simply being close to one another. Its importance in a relationship lies in its capacity to nurture feelings of attraction and desire, creating a dynamic interplay that keeps the relationship vibrant and engaging.

Together, emotional and physical intimacy form a symbiotic relationship, each enhancing and enriching the other. When partners experience both forms of intimacy, they are more likely to cultivate a relationship that is not only deeply satisfying but also resilient in the face of challenges. As we explore the law of intimacy further, we will examine how to cultivate these connections, navigate potential barriers, and ultimately deepen the bonds that bring couples closer together.

In this chapter, we will uncover practical strategies and insights that can help partners explore the multifaceted nature of intimacy, empowering them to forge deeper connections and enhance their love relationships.

Sneha and Siddharth: A Journey of Intimacy

In the vibrant city of Kochi, where the backwaters glisten and the streets are alive with color, Sneha and Siddharth found each other amid the bustling crowds. Their paths crossed during a local art festival, where the air was filled with laughter, music, and the scent of fresh spices. From their first conversation, there was an undeniable spark—an instant connection that felt both exhilarating and comforting.

Building Emotional Intimacy

As their relationship blossomed, Sneha and Siddharth discovered the beauty of emotional intimacy. They spent countless evenings sharing their dreams and fears over steaming cups of chai, sitting on the balcony of Siddharth's cozy apartment. With every conversation, they peeled back the layers of their lives, revealing hopes for the future and the scars of the past.

Sneha confided in Siddharth about her struggles with self-doubt, while Siddharth opened up about his fear of failure. Each revelation deepened their bond, forging a trust that felt unbreakable. They learned to listen—truly listen—to each other, creating a safe haven where vulnerability was not just accepted but cherished. This emotional intimacy became the bedrock of their relationship, allowing them to navigate challenges with resilience and understanding.

Exploring Physical Intimacy

As their emotional connection deepened, Sneha and Siddharth naturally began to explore physical intimacy. Their moments of closeness evolved from innocent touches to gentle embraces that spoke volumes. One evening, under a canopy of stars on a moonlit beach, Siddharth took Sneha's hand and pulled her close, wrapping her in a warm embrace. In that moment, the world around them faded, and it was just the two of them—hearts beating in unison.

With each shared kiss and tender touch, they found themselves more in tune with each other's desires and comfort levels. They understood that physical intimacy was not merely about passion; it was an expression of love, trust, and respect. Whether it was the warmth of a hug after a long day or the thrill of stolen kisses, every moment they shared was a testament to their growing closeness.

The Interplay of Intimacy

As time went on, Sneha and Siddharth learned that emotional and physical intimacy were intricately intertwined. Their emotional connection enhanced their physical experiences, and vice versa. A heartfelt conversation could ignite a spark that transformed a simple kiss into an electrifying expression of love. They celebrated each other's bodies with the same reverence they held for each other's hearts.

One rainy evening, as they watched the downpour from Siddharth's window, they found themselves lost in a moment of laughter and playfulness. In that instant, the joy of their emotional intimacy spilled over into a dance of playful nudges and spontaneous kisses, blurring the lines between laughter and love. The rain outside became a backdrop to their growing passion, a reminder of how their love was a beautiful blend of warmth and excitement.

A Stronger Connection

Through their journey, Sneha and Siddharth discovered that intimacy was not just about moments of closeness but also about the commitment to nurture that bond. They learned to communicate openly about their needs and desires, ensuring that both emotional and physical aspects of their relationship were equally valued.

In moments of disagreement, they relied on their emotional intimacy to guide them. Instead of allowing misunderstandings to create distance, they chose to confront their issues with honesty and compassion. This commitment to open communication only strengthened their connection, reinforcing the trust they had built.

A Love That Flourishes

As their relationship flourished, Sneha and Siddharth embraced the beauty of intimacy in all its forms. They created a rhythm of shared experiences—traveling to new places, cooking meals together, and exploring the art scene in Kochi.

Each adventure brought them closer, filling their lives with laughter and cherished memories.

In the heart of Kochi, amidst the hustle and bustle, Sneha and Siddharth's love story became a testament to the law of intimacy. They learned that the journey of love is not merely about grand gestures but about the quiet moments of connection that build a strong and beautiful relationship.

In the end, it was their deep emotional intimacy that allowed their physical connection to flourish, creating a love that was both passionate and profound. Together, they danced through life, forever intertwined in a beautiful tapestry of trust, respect, and love—proving that true intimacy is the essence of a lasting relationship.

Building Intimacy Through Vulnerability

Intimacy in a relationship is not solely about physical closeness; it thrives on emotional connection, which is often nurtured through vulnerability. Sharing fears, dreams, and insecurities fosters a deep sense of understanding and trust between partners, enhancing their closeness in meaningful ways.

The Power of Sharing Fears

When partners openly share their fears, they create a safe space where both individuals can confront their vulnerabilities together. This act of openness allows them to feel seen and heard, diminishing the weight of their fears. For instance, if one partner expresses anxiety about their career path, the other can offer support and reassurance, fostering a sense of partnership in facing life's challenges.

This mutual sharing cultivates empathy, as partners come to understand each other's struggles. Rather than feeling isolated in their fears, they experience a sense of solidarity, which strengthens their emotional bond.

The Importance of Sharing Dreams

Discussing dreams—whether they are aspirations for the future or simple desires for the relationship—can significantly enhance intimacy. When partners articulate their dreams, they not only share their hopes but also invite their significant other into their inner world. This sharing fosters a sense of teamwork and collaboration, as they can support each other in pursuing these goals.

For example, a partner who dreams of traveling the world can inspire the other to explore new horizons, leading to shared experiences that deepen their connection. By aligning their dreams, couples create a shared vision for their future, reinforcing their commitment and connection.

Navigating Insecurities Together

Insecurities often create barriers in relationships, but discussing them can dissolve these obstacles. When partners share their insecurities—be it about self-worth, appearance, or past experiences—they break down the walls that often isolate individuals in their struggles. This openness encourages reassurance and validation, as partners can affirm each other's worth and beauty.

By confronting insecurities together, couples foster a culture of acceptance and love. When one partner feels insecure, the other's supportive response can bolster confidence and create a stronger emotional bond. This shared vulnerability enhances trust, allowing both individuals to feel safe and supported in expressing their authentic selves.

The Cycle of Vulnerability and Intimacy

The process of sharing fears, dreams, and insecurities creates a positive feedback loop. As partners engage in vulnerability, they experience increased closeness, which encourages further openness. This cycle strengthens the relationship, making it more resilient to challenges.

For instance, a couple that regularly engages in deep conversations about their feelings and experiences will naturally become more attuned to each other's emotional states. This heightened awareness fosters a deeper understanding of each other's needs, leading to a more satisfying and fulfilling relationship.

Building intimacy through vulnerability is a transformative journey that allows partners to connect on a profound level. By sharing fears, dreams, and insecurities, couples cultivate empathy, trust, and a shared sense of purpose. This emotional closeness not only enhances the bond between partners but also creates a strong foundation for navigating life's ups and downs together. Ultimately, it is

this shared vulnerability that weaves the fabric of a resilient and loving relationship, making it richer and more fulfilling.

Maintaining Intimacy Over Time: Tips for Keeping the Spark Alive

Intimacy in a relationship can evolve over time, but with intention and effort, couples can keep the spark alive. Here are some practical tips for maintaining emotional and physical intimacy, including the importance of regular check-ins.

1. Regular Check-Ins

Make it a habit to have regular conversations about your relationship, focusing specifically on intimacy. This can be a designated time each week or month where both partners share their feelings, desires, and any concerns. Ask open-ended questions like:

How are we doing in terms of emotional connection?

Are there any areas where you feel we could improve our intimacy?

What makes you feel most loved and connected?

These discussions create a safe space for both partners to express their needs and desires, helping to address issues before they escalate.

2. Prioritize Quality Time

Amid busy schedules, it's easy to let intimacy take a backseat. Schedule regular date nights or special activities that allow you to focus on each other without distractions. Whether it's a candlelight dinner, a weekend getaway, or simply a walk in the park, dedicating time to one another nurtures connection.

3. Explore New Activities Together

Trying new things can reignite excitement and intimacy. Consider taking a class together, going on an adventure, or engaging in a new hobby. Shared experiences foster connection and create lasting memories, enhancing both emotional and physical intimacy.

4. Express Affection Daily

Small gestures of affection can go a long way in maintaining intimacy. Make it a point to show physical affection daily—whether it's holding hands, hugging, or leaving sweet notes for each other. These little acts reinforce your bond and remind each other of your love.

5. Communicate Openly About Needs

As individuals grow and change, so do their needs and desires. Encourage open dialogue about what intimacy looks like for both of you, and be willing to adapt. If one partner expresses a need for more affection or emotional connection, address it with understanding and care.

6. Celebrate Milestones

Recognizing and celebrating milestones in your relationship, whether big or small, can strengthen your bond. Acknowledge anniversaries, personal achievements, or even just the completion of a challenging week together. Celebrating these moments reinforces your connection and reminds you both of the journey you're on together.

7. Practice Vulnerability

Continue to share your thoughts, fears, and dreams with each other. Being vulnerable deepens emotional intimacy and fosters trust. Create an environment where both partners feel safe to express themselves without fear of judgment.

8. Keep the Physical Connection Alive

Physical intimacy can sometimes wane over time, but it's crucial for maintaining a strong relationship. Make an effort to prioritize physical affection and explore each other's desires. Schedule intimate moments and ensure that both partners feel comfortable expressing their needs.

9. Stay Playful and Spontaneous

Injecting playfulness into your relationship can rekindle the spark. Surprise each other with spontaneous acts of kindness or playful banter. Laughter and fun can keep the relationship dynamic and exciting, making intimacy feel effortless.

10. Reflect on Your Journey Together

Take time to reflect on your relationship's journey—both the highs and lows. Share what you appreciate about each other and the moments that have brought you closer. This reflection reinforces your commitment and reminds you of the love that has endured over time.

Maintaining intimacy over time requires effort, communication, and a willingness to grow together. By implementing regular check-ins, prioritizing quality time, and nurturing both emotional and physical connections, couples can keep the spark alive. Remember, intimacy is a continuous journey, and investing in it can lead to a deeper, more fulfilling relationship.

The Law of Intimacy in Love Relationships

As we conclude our exploration of the law of intimacy in love relationships, it is clear that true intimacy is a multifaceted journey, woven together by threads of emotional and physical connection. The ability to share fears, dreams, and insecurities not only deepens our understanding of one another but also strengthens the very foundation upon which our relationships are built.

By embracing vulnerability, we invite our partners into our innermost worlds, fostering a bond that transcends mere companionship. This deep emotional intimacy, coupled with the warmth of physical affection, creates a harmonious interplay that keeps love alive and vibrant. Regular check-ins, shared experiences, and intentional acts of connection serve as vital practices that nurture and sustain this closeness over time.

As you embark on your own intimacy-building journey, remember that it requires effort, communication, and a willingness to grow together. Every conversation, every shared laugh, and every moment of vulnerability enriches your relationship, making it more resilient in the face of challenges.

Ultimately, the law of intimacy teaches us that love is not just a feeling but a continuous commitment to nurture and cherish each other. By prioritizing intimacy in all its forms, you lay the groundwork for a lasting, fulfilling partnership— one that is not only beautiful but also profoundly meaningful. Embrace this journey, and watch your love flourish in ways you never thought possible

The Eternal Dance of Love

As we reach the end of this journey through the Laws of Love, we find ourselves standing at the intersection of wisdom and action—where the principles of love, connection, and mutual respect come to life. These laws are not mere rules or guidelines; they are the very essence of how we build and nurture relationships that withstand the tests of time. Each law, like a note in a symphony, plays its part in creating the harmony of love that we all seek.

Let us take a moment to Reflect on the profound wisdom we've explored:

The Symphony of Communication

Every word spoken, every silence shared, and every gesture exchanged serves as a bridge or a pause in the intricate symphony of communication. When we speak with care and listen with intention, we create a flow of understanding that allows love to blossom.

The Art of Conflict Resolution

Conflict is inevitable in any relationship, but it is not something to fear. In every conflict lies an opportunity for deeper understanding and connection. The ability to resolve disagreements with respect, empathy, and a shared commitment to the relationship strengthens the bond and fosters growth.

The Pillar of Respect

Respect is the quiet force that strengthens the foundation of any relationship. It is the deep acknowledgment of each other's humanity, and when respect is present, love finds the freedom to grow in beautiful and unexpected ways.

The Essence of Trust

Trust is the heartbeat of love—a quiet, unshakable certainty that we can rely on each other. It is built over time, layer by layer, and once established, it gives love the stability it needs to flourish, even in the face of life's challenges.

Moments that Matter: Quality Time

Love is woven together in moments—small, meaningful, shared experiences. Quality time, where we give each other our undivided attention, creates the fabric of connection that binds us together in profound ways.

The Power of Appreciation

Gratitude is the secret ingredient that transforms the ordinary into the extraordinary. By appreciating one another in the everyday moments, we create a life rich with love, laughter, and shared memories.

The Gift of Support

In every relationship, there will be times of challenge. True love is found in the strength to rise together, offering support, encouragement, and a steady hand through life's ups and downs.

The Art of Compromise

Love is a dance—a dance of give and take. The art of compromise isn't about sacrificing your needs, but about finding a rhythm where both partners feel valued and heard. It's about stepping lightly and harmoniously for each other's happiness.

The Beauty of Individuality

Love thrives when two unique individuals come together, each with their own passions, dreams, and quirks. Celebrating individuality within a partnership not only strengthens the bond but nurtures growth and freedom for both partners.

The Grace of Forgiveness

Forgiveness is the key that unlocks the heart, releasing the weight of past hurts and allowing love to heal. It is an act of grace, a conscious decision to let go of resentment and create space for growth and understanding.

The Language of Love

Love speaks in many languages. Whether through words, acts of service, touch, or gifts, understanding and speaking your partner's love language is the key to nurturing emotional connection and intimacy.

The Depth of Empathy

Empathy is the bridge between hearts. To truly understand your partner's feelings and perspective is to love them in the deepest way possible. It is in empathy that we connect on a soul level, creating a love that is compassionate and enduring.

The Light of Honesty

Honesty is the beacon that guides us through the storms of life. In truth, we find clarity, trust, and the strength to face challenges together. When honesty is embraced, it fosters an atmosphere of openness and mutual respect.

The Journey of Growth

Love is not static; it is a journey of continuous growth. In love, we evolve, we learn, and we blossom. By nurturing each other's growth, we create a partnership that is dynamic, resilient, and full of potential.

The Warmth of Intimacy

Intimacy is the sacred space where souls connect. It is in vulnerability, closeness, and shared moments of true connection that love reaches its deepest expression. Intimacy is the heartbeat of love, where the essence of who we are can be seen, felt, and cherished.

These laws of love are not mere concepts; they are living principles that, when applied with intention and care, have the power to transform relationships. Love, at its core, is about building a partnership grounded in mutual respect, trust, and understanding. It is about creating a space where both individuals can thrive, grow, and share in the beautiful journey of life together.

As you continue your own journey through love, remember that relationships, like all living things, require nurturing. They grow stronger through communication, empathy, support, and the willingness to evolve. There will be moments of joy, and there will be challenges, but with these laws as your guide, you are equipped to navigate the complexities of love with grace, understanding, and an open heart.

May you find the wisdom to live these laws in every relationship you encounter, and may your love always be a reflection of the depth and beauty you bring to the world.

As you close the pages of this book, remember that the true power of the laws of love lies not in their understanding, but in their application. It's easy to read about love, to learn the principles that guide us toward deeper connection and fulfillment. But the real magic happens when we actively choose to live these laws every day—in our words, our actions, and our hearts.

Love is not a passive experience. It is a living, breathing force that requires our conscious participation. Every relationship, no matter how strong, will face challenges. But it is in those moments—when communication falters, when trust is tested, when conflict arises—that the laws of love become your greatest allies.

Now is the time to take action. Here's how:

1.Start with small, intentional steps. Choose one or two laws that resonate with you the most and begin practicing them today. Maybe it's the art of active listening from The Symphony of Communication, or offering genuine appreciation from The Power of Appreciation. Whatever it is, start

2. Make them your daily habits.

Love thrives when we make it a priority. Take a moment each day to practice the principles you've learned. Whether it's setting aside quality time with your partner, expressing gratitude, or speaking with kindness and respect, these small actions, repeated daily, will create a foundation for lasting connection. Love isn't something that happens in big moments alone—it's built in the quiet, everyday choices that shape our relationships.

3. Embrace the challenge of growth.

It's easy to get comfortable in love, but growth comes when we step outside our comfort zone. Don't shy away from difficult conversations or conflicts. See them as opportunities for growth, deeper understanding, and intimacy. The laws of conflict resolution and forgiveness are your tools for navigating these moments. When you face them with an open heart and a willingness to learn, your relationship will be strengthened, not weakened.

4. Be patient with yourself and your partner.

The laws of love are not about perfection; they are about progress. It's okay if you don't always get it right.

Relationships are a journey, and each day presents an opportunity to become better, to love deeper, and to communicate more clearly. Be patient with your growth, and show the same grace to your partner. Love is a continual process of learning, adjusting, and evolving together.

5. Cultivate self-awareness and self-love.

Before you can fully embrace the laws of love in your relationship, you must first practice them with yourself. The Law of Individuality reminds us that love begins within. Take time to know yourself, honor your needs, and practice self-compassion. When you show up as your best self, you'll be able to show up fully for your partner.

6. Let the laws guide you through the storms.

When the inevitable difficulties arise—whether it's a misunderstanding, a personal challenge, or an external stressor—remember that these laws are your compass. They offer you clarity and direction, even in the most turbulent times. Use the tools of honesty, empathy, and compromise to find your way back to each other. Trust that love, built on these principles, is resilient enough to weather any storm.

7. Celebrate your progress.

Don't wait for the big, dramatic moments to celebrate your relationship. Celebrate the small victories—the moments when you communicate openly, when you practice forgiveness, or when you navigate a challenge with empathy and respect. These are the moments that truly define a healthy, loving relationship. Celebrate them, and allow yourself to feel proud of the work you're doing to build a stronger, more loving partnership.

Final Words of Encouragement

You have the wisdom of these laws at your fingertips, but their true value comes from putting them into practice. Love is not something that happens to us—it is something we create, nurture, and protect with intention. The more you apply these laws in your relationship, the more deeply you will experience the beauty, joy, and fulfillment that love has to offer.

Remember: relationships are not about perfection, they're about connection. They're about showing up for each other, learning from each other, and growing together. There will be moments of challenge, but with each one, you will find new depths of understanding and love. By living these laws, you are not just building a relationship—you're building a life filled with meaning, joy, and lasting connection.

So, go forward with confidence. Let these laws be your guide, and let love be the journey that continues to unfold, every day, in ways more beautiful than you ever imagined.

And remember, the most beautiful love stories are the ones written over time, with patience, commitment, and a whole lot of heart.

A Heartfelt Thank You

As you reach the final pages of this book, I want to take a moment to express my deepest gratitude to you, the reader. Thank you for choosing this book, for committing your time and energy to exploring the laws that can deepen and strengthen your relationships. In a world that often moves too quickly, your willingness to pause, reflect, and learn about the art of love is both admirable and inspiring.

By dedicating yourself to this journey, you've already taken a powerful step toward creating lasting, meaningful connections in your life. The fact that you've chosen to invest in yourself and your relationships speaks volumes about your commitment to growth, to understanding, and to love. It is an honor to be a part of that journey with you.

Thank you for trusting us to be your guide in this exploration of love. Your openness to learn and embrace new insights is the very heart of what makes a relationship thrive. I hope that the principles shared in this book have resonated with you, sparked new ideas, and perhaps even inspired you to approach your relationships with a fresh perspective.

Every page was written with the intention of helping you create more meaningful connections and to equip you with the tools to navigate love with grace, patience, and intention. And it is my deepest hope that as you apply the laws of love in your life, you will not only transform your relationships but also experience the kind of love that nourishes, supports, and uplifts you in every season of life.

Thank you for choosing to invest in the beautiful, complex, and rewarding journey of love. It's a privilege to have shared this time with you, and I have no doubt that the love you cultivate from here will be deeper, more fulfilling, and more enduring than you ever imagined.

Wishing you endless love, growth, and connection as you move forward with the tools and insights you've gained. You are worthy of all the love and happiness the world has to offer, and I am so grateful to have been a part of your journey.

The end